STARTING TO

Other How To Books on Business and Management

Arranging Insurance
Be a Freelance Sales Agent
Buy & Run a Shop
Buy & Run a Small Hotel
Buying a Personal Computer
Cash from Your Computer
Collecting a Debt
Communicate at Work
Conduct Staff Appraisals
Conducting Effective Interviews
Doing Business Abroad
Do Your Own Advertising
Do Your Own PR
Employ & Manage Staff
Investing in People
Investing in Stocks & Shares
Keep Business Accounts
Manage a Sales Team
Manage an Office
Manage Computers at Work
Manage People at Work
Managing Budgets & Cash Flows
Managing Meetings

Managing Yourself
Market Yourself
Master Book-Keeping
Master Public Speaking
Mastering Business English
Organising Effective Training
Prepare a Business Plan
Publish a Book
Publish a Newsletter
Raise Business Finance
Sell Your Business
Start a Business from Home
Start Your Own Business
Starting to Manage
Successful Mail Order Marketing
Taking on Staff
Understand Finance at Work
Use the Internet
Winning Presentations
Write a Report
Write & Sell Computer Software
Writing Business Letters
Your Own Business in Europe

Further titles in preparation

The How To Series now contains more than 150 titles in the following categories:

Business Basics
Family Reference
Jobs & Careers
Living & Working Abroad
Student Handbooks
Successful Writing

Please send for a free copy of the latest catalogue for full details
(see back cover for address).

BUSINESS BASICS

STARTING TO MANAGE

How to prepare yourself for a more responsible role at work

Julie-Ann Amos

How To Books

By the same author in this series

Managing Yourself

Cartoons by Mike Flanagan

British Library Cataloguing in Publication data
A catalogue record for this book is available from the British Library.

First published in 1996 by How To Books Ltd, Plymbridge House, Estover Road, Plymouth PL6 7PZ, United Kingdom. Tel: (01752) 202301. Fax: (01752) 202331.

Note: The material contained in this book is set out in good faith for general guidance and no liability can be accepted for loss or expense incurred as a result of relying in particular circumstances on statements made in the book. The laws and regulations are complex and liable to change, and readers should check the current position with the relevant authorities before making personal arrangements.

Produced for How To Books by Deer Park Productions.
Typeset by Kestrel Data, Exeter.
Printed and bound in Great Britain by Cromwell Press,
Broughton Gifford, Melksham, Wiltshire.

Contents

List of Illustrations

Preface

This book has been written for people who are just starting out as managers. It doesn't include large sections on the various management theories—instead, it concentrates on how to manage. This means things like what to do, what to think about, and what to be aware of.

Each chapter includes some common questions and answers, and has a checklist to remind you of the main points. There are also mini case studies, in which you meet fictional characters illustrating some points from the chapter—usually how *not* to do it! Lastly, at the end of each chapter you will find some discussion points, to help you apply what you have learned from the text to your own work situation.

I hope you will find the book useful, and that in time, it will help you become a good manager.

Julie-Ann Amos

IS THIS YOU?

Trainee   Supervisor

Section leader

Business student   Production assistant

Sales executive

Job applicant   Accountant

Works/factory manager

College leaver   University graduate

Transport officer

Retailer   Business owner

Catering manager

Teacher   Health official

College staff

Hotelier   Office worker

Voluntary work organiser

Customer services manager   Training officer

Project leader

Instructor   Construction manager

Youth organiser

Police officer   Fire officer

Prison officer

Social worker   Military leader

Team leader

Practice manager   Marketing manager

1
Understanding Management

ARE YOU A MANAGER?

Most dictionaries define management as 'being in charge of', 'controlling', or 'administering'. Basically, you are a manager if you have a measure of control over any of the following:

- time
- workloads
- decisions
- technology
- equipment
- money
- standards
- meetings
- other people.

Outside of work everyone is a manager, because everyone manages their own life: money, time and decisions. But in work, we often don't think of ourselves as a manager until we have some form of control and/or authority over other people.

MANAGING OR SUPERVISING?

Supervising
The word supervisor comes from the latin words

'super' = over

and

'visor' = to see.

Thus, 'supervisor' = overseer. A supervisor's job is to oversee one or more of the list of things above: to inspect and monitor them.

Managing

A manager has a wider picture. Not only do they inspect and monitor things now, but it is also usually their job to make predictions, to plan ahead, and to decide how things will change and develop. Also, a manager also generally reviews the past when planning and forecasting the future. Thus, the difference between the two is perhaps their viewpoints: the supervisor is often mainly concerned with the present, and the manager with future, present and past.

WHAT DO MANAGERS DO?

There are many functions a manager carries out. A sample of these are:

- control
- taking responsibility
- setting objectives and/or goals
- organisation
- delegation
- accepting authority
- decision-making
- support
- communications
- training
- monitoring/evaluating
- leadership
- motivation
- planning.

The list is not exhaustive: how many more can you think of?

BALANCING MANAGEMENT

Imagine you are shipwrecked. There are a dozen of you in a liferaft, looking for land. You are elected to stand at the front of the boat, keeping a good lookout for land. After a long hard day of your colleagues rowing, you can see land on the horizon, and you encourage them to row towards it as hard as they can. However, when you get closer, you realise three things:

- There are rocks and reefs between you and the land.

- A strong tide is threatening to sweep you off course, and straight past the land.

- Your shipmates are dangerously tired now, and may not have the strength to reach the land unless you take an oar yourself, and help them row. What is more, they are beginning to grumble nastily about you 'not pulling your weight', and leaving them to do all the work.

So, what do you do? For here you have it in a nutshell: the balancing act that is management. Do you pitch in and help the others, and risk losing the overview (which only you fully understand)? Or, do you stay in control and risk alienating the workforce? One thing is certain; the decision isn't straightforward or easy.

WEIGHING UP THE OPTIONS

Most managerial functions operate in pairs, and a manager needs to balance the two extremes, leaning towards one or the other as and when appropriate. On the following pages you will see some of the main balances of management illustrated in Figures 1 to 7. These are:

- Control v. motivation

- Procedures v. flexibility

- Progress v. stability

- Delegation v. personal control

- Responsibility v. authority

- Security v. risk-taking

- Logic v. inspiration.

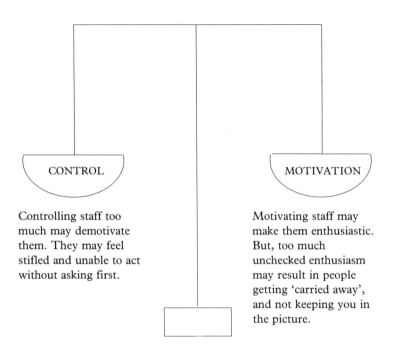

Fig. 1. Control v. motivation.

Hard, isn't it? We want, as managers, to do all these things, but to balance them so we don't focus too much on any one thing and suffer as a result of ignoring its partner.

QUESTIONS AND ANSWERS

So is balancing management about 'sitting on the fence'?
Not at all. No one is suggesting that you 'sit on the fence' at all times and keep balanced exactly in the middle. Nobody has an equal balance of everything: we all have natural tendencies—for example, to favour progress and change, or to prefer stability and the status quo. What is important is realising that your usual way of doing things is not the only way, neither will it always be appropriate.

So how does this help me be a better manager?
By learning about good management. Read this book and others—a useful list of further reading can be found at the back of this book.

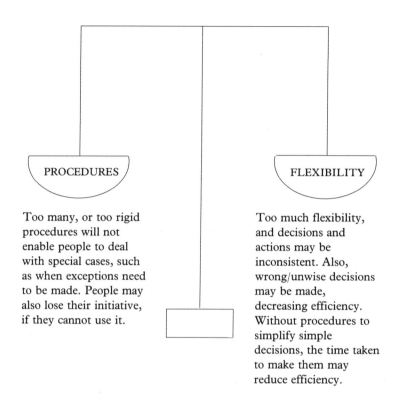

PROCEDURES

FLEXIBILITY

Too many, or too rigid procedures will not enable people to deal with special cases, such as when exceptions need to be made. People may also lose their initiative, if they cannot use it.

Too much flexibility, and decisions and actions may be inconsistent. Also, wrong/unwise decisions may be made, decreasing efficiency. Without procedures to simplify simple decisions, the time taken to make them may reduce efficiency.

Fig. 2. Procedures v. flexibility.

Look at yourself and where you work. See how things, could be improved, and also where things are working well. Use what you read to help you make changes to your approach and the way you do things, where you can.

So do I need to learn about management theories to manage well?
Not necessarily. They can help you understand what is happening at work, and why, and how things might be improved. But you need to remember that a theory is just that—a *theory*. A theory is an idea, not a fact, and therefore it may not work for you, in your place of work. For this reason, wherever possible, this book concentrates on practical ways of doing things, rather than theories.

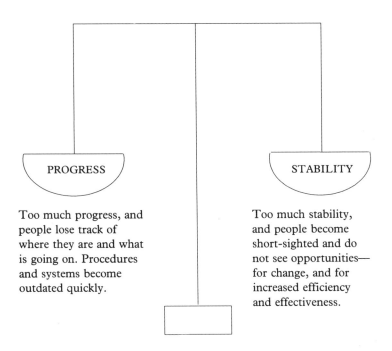

PROGRESS

STABILITY

Too much progress, and
people lose track of
where they are and what
is going on. Procedures
and systems become
outdated quickly.

Too much stability,
and people become
short-sighted and do
not see opportunities—
for change, and for
increased efficiency
and effectiveness.

Fig. 3. Progress v. stability.

RECOGNISING MANAGEMENT STYLES

Your style of managing will depend on four main influences:

1. yourself

2. other people working with or around you

3. the situation

4. constraints imposed by your organisation and/or workplace.

You may have one style which you tend naturally to adopt, or
your style may vary depending on how the mixture of the four
ingredients varies. However, there seem to be six main styles of
management.

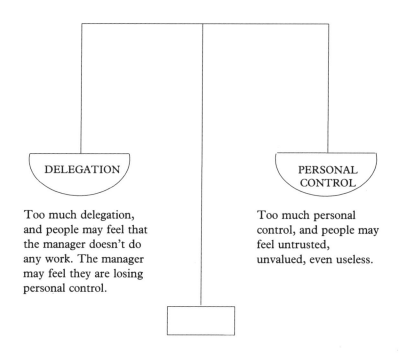

Fig. 4. Delegation v. personal control.

CHOOSING A MANAGEMENT STYLE

Being authoritarian

The *authoritarian* manager dictates, and tells people what to do.

Good points
● People submit to the manager's leadership.

● The manager is always in control.

Bad points
● People are dependent on the manager.

● People are insecure, unproductive, and have little or no initiative without the manager.

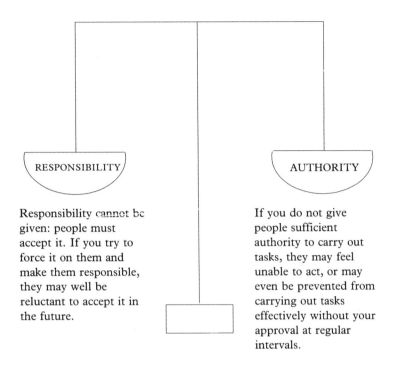

RESPONSIBILITY

AUTHORITY

Responsibility cannot be given: people must accept it. If you try to force it on them and make them responsible, they may well be reluctant to accept it in the future.

If you do not give people sufficient authority to carry out tasks, they may feel unable to act, or may even be prevented from carrying out tasks effectively without your approval at regular intervals.

Fig. 5. Responsibility v. authority.

Being persuading

A manager with a *persuading* style is like a parent in the way they treat people. They make the decisions, and then try to persuade people that this is the best course of action.

Good points

- People generally feel less dominated than with an authoritarian manager.

- Some people may like this level of control and care.

Bad points

- Some people may resent the manager, as they are not treated as adults.

- The manager may feel hurt if people fail, as if they have been 'let down'.

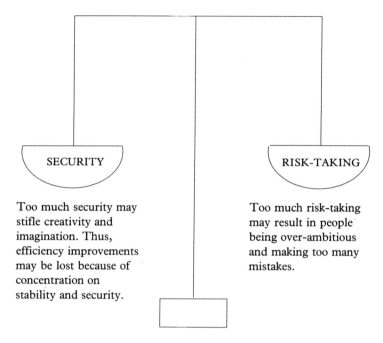

Fig. 6. Security v. risk-taking.

Too much security may stifle creativity and imagination. Thus, efficiency improvements may be lost because of concentration on stability and security.

Too much risk-taking may result in people being over-ambitious and making too many mistakes.

Being consulting

With a *consulting* manager, people are welcome to contribute ideas, suggestions etc, and the manager discusses these and then makes the decision.

Good points
● People feel involved.

● People feel part of a team, and feel valued.

Bad points
● People may resent decisions if their own suggestions were un-successful.

● People may try to challenge the manager's decision.

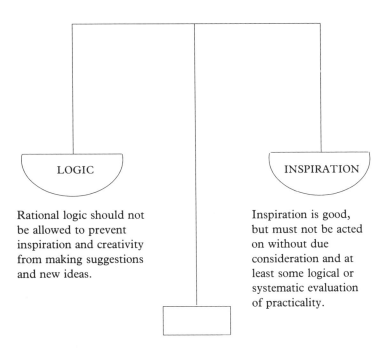

Fig. 7. Logic v. inspiration.

Being democratic

With a *democratic* manager, the manager and others all take part in work. Decisions are made by the whole group, and the manager agrees to abide by these, as long as they are within any boundaries or constraints imposed by the workplace and/or organisation.

Good points
- Individuals feel enthusiastic, and tend to take responsibility readily.

- Communication and teamwork are good.

Bad points
- The manager needs to have complete confidence in people.

- The manager can lose control.

Being a delegator

The *delegating* manager sets limits, and gives problems, work etc to others. They refer back on difficulties, but otherwise take on the entire task as their own.

Good points
- Work is efficient.

- Individuals are given experience of a wide variety of work.

Bad points
- Individuals may feel overburdened with responsibility.

- The manager may not be available to help when problems arise.

Being an abdicator

The manager *abdicates*—opts out—by becoming so involved in their own work that others are left to their own devices. Often, managers do this, because they mistakenly think they are delegating.

Good points
- The manager is free to get on with their own work.

Bad points
- People blame the manager, even when it is their own fault.

- Work is poor, morale is low, and people feel frustrated and resentful.

CHECKLIST

- Be aware that management is a balancing act.

- Try to avoid too narrow a focus on any one thing.

- Aim for an appropriate style, without being too authoritarian, or abdicating.

- Always try to remember: how would you feel if your boss behaved exactly like you?

CASE STUDIES—AN INTRODUCTION

Let us introduce you to three managers whom you will be looking at in the following chapters. Each is different, and has gained their present position via a different route. We will observe how they handle a variety of situations.

Bev Hall, Shift Manager

Bev Hall is in her late forties, and has worked at the same nursing home on the south coast for twelve years. Before that, she worked in other similar homes for the elderly. She has never received any management or supervisory training, but because of her age and experience, has always been looked to for advice by other staff. A year ago, a new Matron made changes to the organisation of the home, and Bev was made Shift Manager. She now has management responsibility for twelve Care Assistants, two Domestics, plus a cook. She feels that these resent her new position, and does not like having an office to work in, rather than being 'out and about'.

Nikki Coates, Office Manager

Nikki Coates is twenty-two, and recently gained an internal promotion to the busy head office of a large retail company. She is friendly, and seems to 'get on' well with her staff of five, but sometimes worries as to whether she is managing the office as well as it could be managed. Her predecessor had a management qualification, and although Nikki has a qualification in Administration, she feels it did not prepare her for dealing with the day-to-day difficulties of managing a hectic office.

Mike Summers, Corporate Accounting Manager

Mike Summers is a graduate. Having gained his university degree in Accountancy, he gained his first job as manager of a four-strong Corporate Accounts section of a local authority. Three of his staff are studying for their accountancy qualifications by day release or correspondence course, and he is aware that although he is better qualified, they know far more about the section and how it works than he does. He feels that he needs to take control of the team, and stamp his authority on it, if he is to be respected and taken seriously.

DISCUSSION POINTS

1. Think of a good manager you have known. Why were they good?

2. Think of a bad manager you have known. Have you ever done any of the things you didn't like about *their* management?

3. Which management style fits you most of the time? Could this be improved on?

2
Managing Workloads

MANAGING TIME

Time cannot be managed. It can't be increased or decreased, delegated, reallocated, saved or lost. Everybody, no matter who they are, has the same amount of it available to them every day. What is more, it is one of the few things in this world that you can waste, misuse, throw away or lose without it bearing a grudge—tomorrow you will still get the same amount of it, no matter how badly you spend it today.

What you can't do, however, is turn back the clock and get back what you lost or wasted yesterday.

BEING EFFECTIVE AND EFFICIENT

Management is about both effectiveness and efficiency. Good time management means we aim to be both. However, it is important to realise that they are not the same.

EFFECTIVE = Doing the right things

EFFICIENT = Doing something in the right way

You can be both, neither, or just one, as the table in Fig. 8 shows. First, we are going to look at how to be **effective:** how to make sure we do the right things, and don't spend our time doing the wrong ones. That may sound rather basic, but very rarely do we actually look at *what* we do—our effectiveness. Many people spend far more time looking at efficiency—*how* we do things, and ways of doing things in the best way. The rest of the book will help you there, but first, let's take a look at effectiveness.

RECORDING YOUR TIME

You cannot improve how you spend your time unless you know what

	EFFECTIVE	NOT EFFECTIVE
EFFICIENT	Doing the right things in the right way, or well	Doing the wrong things well
NOT EFFICIENT	Doing the right things in the wrong way, or badly	Doing the wrong things badly

Fig. 8. Efficiency or effectiveness?

you spend it on. So, you need to measure what you are spending your time doing at present. Keep a time log for at least ten working days, preferably a month. In this, you will list everything you do and for how long. Include all those cups of coffee and telephone calls both made and received—everything you do.

At the end of the recording period, do some sums on where your time went. Analyse how much time was spent on each activity. When you have the totals, you may well be surprised at just how much of your time certain things take.

Ask yourself some general questions, and try to be objective and honest about the results:

1. What time of day did I get the most achieved? What time of day did I get the least achieved?

2. How much time was spent on inefficiency—waiting, looking for things, being interrupted etc?

3. How much time did I spend on tasks that were unnecessary?

4. How much time did I spend on tasks I could or should have got somebody else to do?

5. Did I achieve all the things I needed to? If not, why not?

ASSESSING EFFECTIVENESS

Now, let's take a closer look at that list. If you were to go through your results and make one long list of every single task you did, e.g. making phone calls, answering mail, attending a meeting, writing a report, reading etc, it would tell you what your workload was for the period of the time record.

Make out a list for your current workload. Write down *everything* you have to do, including routine things, and things already started. We are going to work on your workload, and see how effective you are.

Step 1—delegating

'D' stands for delegate. Mark a big 'D' by any activities which shouldn't be done by you. Over a period of time, work towards delegating these to a more appropriate person wherever possible. You may find it easier delegating things you don't like doing, but dislike delegating things you enjoy. Well, there's nothing wrong with keeping a few tasks that are enjoyable but not, strictly speaking, part of your job. Just resist the temptation to keep too many.

Step 2—pruning

Now look for any tasks which really shouldn't be done at all—by anyone. Mark them with an 'X'. Again, over a period of time, you should try to eliminate these wherever possible. There may always be a small number of tasks that your boss or other senior people require you to do that are, in your opinion, unnecessary. You may be stuck with these, but there is no harm in politely pointing out your views.

Step 3—prioritising

Everything that is left unmarked should be done by you, if you have done your list correctly. Now prioritise these. Put an 'A' by tasks that are high priority—essential to your job and objectives, or to the objectives of your organisation. Put a 'B' by medium priority tasks. These are less important than 'A' tasks, and are not essential, although they may be important.

Step 4—identifying lower priorities

Put a 'C' by low priority tasks. These are tasks that are supposed to be done, but would not cause major problems if they weren't. Check carefully to see whether any could be delegated, and change them to a 'D', delegating them if it is possible to.

Step 5—separating the lists

You now have a list of your own tasks. Once you have eliminated the 'X' tasks and the 'D' tasks, these are the only things you should be spending your time on. Separate these remaining tasks into three separate lists—so you have an 'A' list, a 'B' list and a 'C' list. Some managers just operate one list, marking it 'A', 'B' or 'C' as appropriate, but to start with you will probably find it easier to operate three separate lists.

Step 6—choosing an order

So, your highest priority is to get the 'A' tasks done. Or is it? Take a few minutes to go through all three lists, and remember, you have all these tasks to do yourself. For each task, mark items with a 'U' if they are urgent, and an 'I' if they are important. Some tasks will be neither, some will be both: it's rather like effectiveness and efficiency —they are not the same.

ASSESSING IMPORTANCE AND URGENCY

Understanding importance

Important tasks are—guess what?—*important*. That means you need to spend enough time on them to make sure you get them right.

Understanding urgency

Urgent tasks are not necessarily important, so get them out of the way quickly: they usually don't have to be perfect, they just have to be done— *urgently*. Fig. 9 shows the difference between important and urgent tasks.

Deciding on an order

You can see that you obviously need to do tasks marked 'UI' and 'U' first. Are they all on the 'A' list? Probably not. The fact is that just because a task is low priority, it doesn't mean it isn't urgent. So, get it out of the way quickly.

It is largely a matter of personal taste, but a good rule for deciding what order to do tasks in would probably be as follows:

- U tasks—A list, then B, then C

- UI tasks—A list, then B, then C

- I tasks—A list, then B, then C

	URGENT	NOT URGENT
IMPORTANT	'UI'—Important *and* urgent—do immediately, taking sufficient time to get the task done well	'I'—Important, but can wait
NOT IMPORTANT	'U'—do quickly, but spend as little time as possible on these	Leave until last

Fig. 9. Importance or urgency?

● Unmarked tasks remaining

Doesn't it sound simple when you see it like that?

Planning big tasks
Sometimes, tasks are too large to be done at one sitting. So, watch out for this, and when you find such tasks, break them into smaller steps and add these to the lists, coding them appropriately and crossing off the big overall task.

QUESTIONS AND ANSWERS

But this all takes time. Surely if I did all this before starting work I wouldn't have much time left for anything else?
Not at all. You are *investing* time at the beginning, to *save* time later. Your A/B/C lists (let's call them your TO DO lists) only have to be set up once, then you add to them every day, crossing things off as

you complete them. In return for the time invested at the beginning, you will spend less time deciding what to do next, jumping from task to task, dealing with interruptions, or even worrying about how to get it all done. But you must update your lists *every day*: what was not urgent yesterday may have become urgent today.

Won't my lists just keep getting longer and longer?
Yes and no. They will get longer as new tasks are added: every time the telephone rings and a new task comes your way, or the morning post brings more work, you simply add it to your lists. But they get shorter as you complete tasks and cross them off, or delegate them. And just think of all the peace of mind you would get from knowing you can't forget to do something or miss a deadline, because it is all on your list to make sure you remember.

So how do I add in all the new tasks that come my way?
Just add them to the appropriate TO DO list, either A, B or C, and mark them urgent and/or important, then they can be dealt with as appropriate. If possible, carry on and finish the task you are doing before starting any new one, unless it really cannot wait. Also, always remember that a lot of quick, low priority, urgent tasks, such as telephone calls or arranging meetings or appointments, could perhaps be delegated in a block to someone with more time and/or fewer tasks.

SCHEDULING AND DIARISING

So far, we have talked about prioritising and planning, and what order to do tasks in. This was effectiveness—doing the right things in the right order. Scheduling and diarising is one thing that will help you be more **efficient**—doing things well. So how do you decide exactly *when* to do tasks?

Individual tastes vary as to what type of diary is best, and there are many sorts available. There are also many personal organisers which combine diaries with TO DO lists. Whichever you use, the following list of points will be applicable, and will help you use your diary to best advantage.

Practical tips

Scheduling time
Plan and schedule your time on a weekly and daily basis—this means you need to set aside a small amount of time to do this every day, and every week.

Keep some time back
Never schedule all your time—always keep some reserved for urgent tasks that arise.

Update daily
Take a small amount of time *every day* in the morning to update your TO DO lists and preview that day's tasks. Carry forward tasks not completed yesterday, and if you end up with too long a list of tasks for today, delegate some, or move them on in your schedule.

Transfer from TO DO lists to diary
Schedule tasks from your TO DO lists into your diary. This may seem like a waste of time, but it is vital. If you and others see blank space in your diary, you will think you have spare time to take on more tasks. You don't—remember all the things on your lists and more coming your way all the time? So, at the start of every day, use some time to decide which items to do when, and book them into the diary.

This really is important—until now we have decided *what* to do, but now you are making sure you keep the time free to do things *when* they need doing. So remember to book in your scheduling and updating time every morning. Think of it as a meeting between three parties—yourself, your TO DO lists and your diary. If you had an appointment with your boss, you would probably put it in your diary so you would remember it. Well, you have an appointment with a task once it is in your diary—it is a major key to getting things done on time.

Remember timing
Schedule important tasks when you will be at your best. This will be a different time for everyone—some people work better early in the day, others later.

Respect other people's time
Don't be late or break appointments at the last minute unless it is absolutely unavoidable. It disrupts other people's schedules, and they may do the same to you.

Travelling and waiting
Use travelling and waiting time productively—always have something with you that you can do in a spare five minutes, so time isn't wasted.

Routine calls and correspondence
Allow time for making telephone calls and dealing with routine correspondence. Book this time like an appointment—that way you know you will have time to do them.

Setting deadlines
If a task has no deadline, set your own, on the basis of its priority. Then enter it in your diary in the usual way.

AVOIDING STRESS

Stress is a large topic. In the following paragraphs, you will find a few simple pointers about managing workloads that will help you avoid stress.

Practical tips

Meeting deadlines
Meet deadlines wherever possible. Stress is not caused by all the things we do—it is caused by all the work we *don't* do, preying on our minds and building up pressure.

Setting goals
Set realistic goals—accept that you cannot do everything, especially not all at once.

Sleeping
Find out what your minimum sleep requirement is. Make sure you get it. Working too late often means you get insufficient sleep, as you go home after work and try to fit your home life into a shorter space of time. This either makes you pressured at home, which may stop you sleeping, or you may end up staying up longer. Insufficient sleep just means you work slower and less well the next day: it would be more efficient to sleep more and work better.

Taking 'time out'
Always take a little 'time out' to think, listen, relax, take a walk etc—whatever works for you—to unwind from the pressures of the day. Taking a coffee break may do this, but too much caffeine from tea and/or coffee can just 'wind you up' again.

Being realistic
Recognise your limitations, and try not to take on things you either

can't do, or don't have sufficient time to do. Set or agree to realistic goals and deadlines only.

Staying organised
Keep your office or workspace well organised. This doesn't mean tidy, it means *organised*—so both you and others can find things without wasting time and getting into a panic.

Taking time off
Plan holidays and time off well in advance, and stick to them.

UNDERSTANDING DELEGATION

Delegation is giving someone (usually a subordinate) the authority to carry out a task. They are *accountable* for the task, and can make decisions relating to it (within any limits that are set), but the manager keeps the overall responsibility.

Remember effectiveness and efficiency? Well, the most effective managers spend their time doing only the tasks that only they can do. They delegate the rest.

Advantages
● The manager has more time.

● The manager is free for planning, creative work, and for *managing*—which is, after all, what they are paid for.

● Staff are developed—they develop new skills, and use their existing skills fully.

● Staff are involved, and therefore happier and more satisfied in their work.

● Morale is good.

● Decisions are often better, as they are made by the people 'closest to the action'.

● Time is saved. Delays while people wait for your decision are eliminated—they decide for themselves.

● You are protected in the event of absence (holidays, sickness etc) as your work can go on, simply being delegated in your absence.

Disadvantages

● Some managers fear losing control. Avoid this by making the other person's limits of authority clear, and checking on them occasionally.

● Some managers fear the task will be done less well: 'they wouldn't do it as well as me.' Probably not at first, but in time and with help, it will be done just as well as you could, but without you doing any work. Just think of all the time you could save!

● Some staff may constantly refer back, to check things are proceeding satisfactorily. Avoid this by briefing them properly, and try to encourage 'management by exception'. This is where you are not informed if things are going normally, only if things are exceptionally good or bad.

● People may feel 'put upon'. Avoid this by spreading out your delegation. Even if one person is better than the others, do not overload them: delegate to the others, so they have a chance to become good too.

● Some managers are afraid the other person will do a better job than them. Well, good! Let them produce good work, and you do the same with the work *you* are good at. This is efficiency —doing things in the best way.

DELEGATING PROPERLY

Familiarisation
Get to know people—not just what they can do already, but what they would like to learn to do. Try to match delegated tasks to individuals if possible.

Limitations
Know the limits. Ask yourself:

● What do you want?

● To what standard?

● How will you judge or measure the result?

- What are the constraints —time?
                          —money?
                          —resources?
                          —staff?

- How much authority do you give the other person?

- What do you want them to refer back to you on, and when?

Briefing
Brief the other person properly. Tell them the answers to the above list, so they know exactly what's going on.

Authorising
Brief others that you are delegating this task, so they know what authority you have given to the person it is delegated to.

Training
Train people if necessary. This does not have to be a training course—show them, explain, or get them to talk to someone else who has done it before.

Availability
Be available. Don't cut yourself off so people can't ask for help if they need it.

Checking
Check on progress or results as planned. Do not over-check: let people 'get on with it', but check on them at agreed intervals.

CHECKLIST

- Carry out a time-recording exercise periodically, to check you are not developing bad habits.

- Constantly check and update your TO DO list: tasks that are not urgent will become more and more urgent the longer you leave them.

- Take time to prioritise, so you do things in the right order.

- Be sensible—don't subject yourself to unnecessary stress.

- Delegate as much as possible, but taking time to train and brief people properly.

- Try to discourage staff 'delegating upwards' *their* tasks or decisions to you—unless it really is necessary.

- Beware of wasting other people's time, for example by being late. It will only encourage them to do it to you.

- Say 'no' to tasks that shouldn't be yours, and direct them to the appropriate person.

CASE STUDIES

Bev learns that effectiveness is not the same as efficiency

Matron asks Bev to make out duty lists. These are lists of tasks that need to be done by the care assistants. Each list is to be copied and given out at the beginning of the shift, and people will sign it to say they have completed tasks. Bev does this, and the lists are signed each day. After a week, Matron carries out an inspection. 'Bev, the Home is disgraceful!' she says. 'Standards have never been so bad. Whatever is going wrong? You'll have to make sure things improve. I'll inspect again in two days time, and things had better be up to scratch then.'

If only Bev had concentrated more on *how* things were being done (efficiency), and less on *whether* they were being done (effectiveness), this could have been avoided. Staff had been effective but not efficient, so standards had slipped.

Nikki learns about priorities—and responsibilities

Nikki keeps a diary, in which she schedules meetings, deadlines and tasks. She also keeps a record of what her staff are doing. She receives an urgent call one Monday from a senior manager, asking for some figures to go in a management report on Friday. She checks the diary and allocates the work. 'It's not urgent, Bill, but I would like it by the end of the week.' On Wednesday, the computer system breaks down, and work has to be done manually. On Thursday, Nikki speaks to all the staff. 'We've got a day's worth of computer input to catch up on, as well as keeping up with today's work. I want you all to put aside everything that's not urgent until next week, so we can catch up.' Bill therefore leaves the figures—after all, they aren't urgent. On Friday morning, when the manager calls, the figures haven't been done. Nikki feels stupid.

If she had told Bill why the figures were needed and when, he could have prioritised them correctly. But then again, Nikki should have kept an eye on the deadline to make sure Bill was on time—it was ultimately her responsibility.

Mike does too much checking

Mike likes to delegate. He accepts work coming in, and re-allocates it to one of his team, keeping himself free to check and monitor progress. He sets deadlines for progress, and asks regularly how things are going. Over a period of time, he notices that Rachel is producing less accurate and well-presented work. When he asks her about this, she shrugs and says, 'Well, you always check it anyway, so I only do a rough draft.' When he is away at a meeting, some work is sent out with several mistakes. Without him there to check, his staff's work can't be guaranteed to come up to standard. And yet, they're all good people. If only he offered them some responsibility, instead of keeping checking on them every five minutes, they might take on tasks like checking and presenting their work properly.

DISCUSSION POINTS

1. Where did each of the three managers in the case studies go wrong?

2. What things do you do that would be better delegated, or handled differently?

3. Who delegates work to you? Is it all suitable, or would someone else be better placed to do it?

3
Managing Problems and
Making Decisions

LOOKING AT PROBLEMS AND DECISIONS

In this chapter, we will look at decision-making and problem-solving. Of course, not all decisions you make are in answer to a problem —many will be simply a matter of trying to choose the best from a number of alternatives. However, because of the links between decision-making and problem-solving, we will look at them together.

Whenever you have a problem to be solved or an issue to be decided upon, there is a logical sequence you can follow to ensure the right decision is made and implemented.

1. Define the problem or issue.
2. Gather information.
3. Create options.
4. Evaluate options.
5. Make the decision(s).
6. Implement the decision(s).
7. Follow up and evaluate.

DEFINING PROBLEMS OR ISSUES

Whatever the problem or issue is, take some time to think about it. Problems do not solve themselves, nor do decisions make themselves, so do not fall into the trap of leaving things alone and hoping they will sort themselves out. This is *not* 'thinking about it', it is *procrastination*—putting things off—the sign of an ineffectual manager. Simply think the matter through thoroughly.

Define problems or issues carefully, and preferably in writing. The problem you are initially faced with, or the issue that needs a decision, may not actually be at the heart of the matter. Let me explain.

Problems v. solutions
Let's say your boss asks you to improve the accuracy of some

work—there are too many errors. What is the problem? Most people in this situation would say that the problem or issue is how to improve accuracy. Wrong! Improving accuracy is the *solution*—the desired outcome. So what is the problem? You don't know!

Although this may seem a little strange at first, very often you will find that the problem you are faced with is actually a solution. It is then up to you to define the problem. Try drawing a diagram, or writing out a list of possible problems, then find out which is the real one, or the most likely. For example:

Problem	*Solution*
Lack of time	Improved accuracy
Poor standards	
Bored, inattentive staff	
Work too difficult	
Staff poorly trained or untrained	
Unclear objectives	
Poor materials	
Faulty equipment	
etc etc	

From this, you can quickly decide which problem or problems are the cause. Then, specifically define the problem and desired outcome in writing. For example:

Problem—Lack of time and demotivated staff.
Desired outcome—Improved accuracy.

Social v. technical

It is also helpful to remember that most problems or issues have two aspects: social and technical. Think of crabs and lobsters. Crabs and lobsters are both caught in fishing pots, even though their strong claws make them perfectly capable of climbing out. But they don't, so they stay caught! Why? What exactly is the problem? (See Fig. 10.)

Crabs
Crabs try to climb out, scrambling and climbing on and over each other in the process. Sometimes one will succeed, but their problem is that as one crab nears escape, the others will grab it and pull it back down in their own bid for freedom. They just don't co-operate.

Fig. 10. Most problems have a social and technical aspect.

If they left each other alone, they could climb out one at a time. Their problem is **social**.

Lobsters
Lobsters don't even seriously try. They never look up, so they keep trying to find a way out through the side of the pot, and almost never climb up to freedom. Their problem is **technical**.

Consider the previous example. The social part of the problem is that staff are demotivated. The technical part is that they haven't sufficient time to do the job properly. No one is saying that the two things aren't related—one reason why the staff are demotivated may well be because they are rushed, and they know they are producing poor work, but this doesn't have to be the case. Not every single issue or problem you look at will have both social and technical aspects, but a large percentage of them will, so it is worth remembering.

Once you have defined exactly what the problem is, write it down. This will prevent you becoming sidetracked.

GATHERING INFORMATION

You need to find out about things. Perhaps you still can't be sure exactly what the real problem is, until you have done some investigation. Start looking for information about the situation, to help you prepare to create options and make a decision.

Remember the quality of information

When gathering information, always make written notes of what you learn, so it cannot be confused or forgotten. Keep a record of everything, and it is often helpful to remember that the *quality* of information is as important as the *quantity*.

Facts
Facts are things that are known to be true. They are provable and reliable.

Deductions
Deductions (or conclusions) are thoughts based on facts. They are logically derived from and supported by facts, but unlike facts cannot be directly proved, only concluded (if they can be proven, they are a fact, not a deduction). As information, therefore, they do not have the same worth as facts: if you had two pieces of information, one fact and one deduction, the fact should have more importance in your thinking.

Opinions
Opinions are thoughts, based on information which may include facts, but which is not completely factual. An opinion is a belief or judgement, and cannot be proved. As information, opinions are the least important.

Remember the source of information

Also bear in mind the *source* of a piece of information. Something from an original source—'from the horse's mouth'—is more reliable than information which has been passed on via someone else, especially if passed by word of mouth.

Points to remember

Keep in mind the following points when you gather information:

- Do I need more information?

- Does this information lead me to more?

- Have I missed anything?

- Is there a pattern evolving?

- Is the situation social, technical, or both?

You don't need to do lengthy research in books and documents —talking to people is an excellent way of gathering information, and will make people feel they are involved in the decision-making process. This is important, because people are more likely to be helpful and supportive of your decision if they feel they had some part in it.

Time wasting

Don't spend so much time gathering information that you skimp on time to evaluate options and make the decision. Some managers become absorbed in the information, using this as a subconscious means of putting off making a difficult decision—procrastination again.

CREATING OPTIONS

The purpose of creating options is to give you a number of possible options, alternatives or solutions, from which you can make your decision. You do not have to do this alone—you can get several people or a group to look at an issue and generate options. This has the advantage of 'several heads being better than one', and minimises the likelihood of you overlooking something.

The main methods of creating options are logical thinking and creative thinking.

Using logical thinking

Logical thinking is also known as convergent thinking, vertical thinking, analytical thinking or deductive reasoning. It is a process of logical deduction. You take known facts or other information, and draw deductions from them to arrive at a solution.

Advantages
- The solution is beyond doubt the right one.

- Good for solving technical problems.

Disadvantages
- There may be insufficient information to draw conclusions and deductions from.

- There may not be only one right answer.

- The 'right answer' arrived at may not be the *best* answer.

Using creative thinking

Creative thinking uses the imagination to make opinions and deductions from information that may be factual, but may not. It is also known as divergent thinking, lateral thinking or bisociative thinking.

Advantages
- Options can be generated without any facts.

- More options can be generated than by logical thinking.

- More factors can be taken into account.

Disadvantages
- People can find it hard to think creatively, especially when they are used to working analytically.

- Because the options are not always based on facts, they may turn out to be wrong when more facts are known.

- Options and decisions may not be taken seriously by others, without the backup of facts and logic.

Brainstorming

There are several creative thinking techniques, but the most popular is brainstorming—a process of imaginative suggestion. A group of people are encouraged to come up with ideas or suggestions, regardless of how silly or impractical they can be. Ideas are not judged, criticised or evaluated in any way, so people feel free to use their imaginations and be creative. A relaxed, light-hearted atmosphere will encourage people to 'bounce ideas around'.

Record *every* option the group comes up with—even if it is impossibly impractical. This is important, because even ideas that are no good themselves may still be of value, as they may make other ideas occur to people, and these resulting ideas may themselves be useful.

Once a large number of ideas has been generated, they can be evaluated and narrowed down to good suggestions.

Advantages
- Produces a large quantity of options.

- Motivates people.

- Can build working relationships between the people in the group.

Disadvantages
- Some people find it difficult to suspend criticism and judgement.

- The leader of the session must be careful to keep things 'on track'.

- A session can degenerate into a frivolous atmosphere, where people don't take things seriously.

Comparing logical and creative thinking

Logical, analytical thinking often doesn't give imagination a chance. People are often trained in logical thinking at school and other stages in their learning, but rarely in creative thinking. Creative thinking can therefore be difficult for many people.

What are the barriers to creative thinking?

- People think they can't be creative—they have 'mental blocks'.

- People believe there is one right answer.

- People want to conform, so they give options they think will be acceptable or well-received.

- People are lazy—they accept the obvious, and don't look for other options.

- People want to get the issue out of the way, so they evaluate too quickly.

- People are afraid of being 'wrong' and looking foolish.

Encouraging creative thinking

There are four main ways to encourage creative thinking:

1. *Suspend judgement*—give and allow no criticism.

2. '*Freewheel*'—the wilder the ideas the better. Let people come up with anything they want.

3. *Quality not quantity*—the more ideas the better.

4. *Combining*—an idea isn't just left as it is. Combine ideas and build on ideas to make others.

Groups v. individuals

Whether to use a group of people or your own judgement to make decisions is a choice you may face. Each has its own advantages and disadvantages.

Individual problem-solving
- An expert usually knows best.

- It tends to be quicker.

- Individuals tend to have their ideas 'dry up' quicker than groups.

- Narrow thinking can limit the options generated.

- Stress can be high—it is lonely 'carrying the can' for a decision.

Group problem-solving
- Better than average solutions are usually achieved.

- Discussions can get out of hand.

- More ideas can be generated.

- People may be upset if their idea is rejected.

- Solutions can take longer to produce.

- Solutions tend to be more accurate.

QUESTIONS AND ANSWERS

So does it matter which type of thinking I use?
Yes. If there is only one correct answer, or where facts are involved, logical (analytical) thinking is best. But where imagination is required, or to generate options from which you can choose the *best* answer, creative thinking is best.

Why is it sometimes so hard to think of options?
Because creativity and imagination are brain functions which are

Table 1. Looking at options

Option	Advantages	Disadvantages	Likely results
1. Reduce workload	Reduces time pressure	Less work done. Staff may get bored	More accurate work but less of it!
2. Train staff	Increases work accuracy, Staff able to cope with time pressures	Takes time. May cost	Increased accuracy
3. Give incentives or bonus schemes	Improved staff morale and motivation	Costs money May demotivate those unable to achieve bonuses	May improve accuracy, but cause conflict
4. Introduce accuracy checks	Will 'weed out' inaccurate work	Takes time. May antagonise staff. Won't improve work, just remove substandard work	Increased accuracy, but decreased amount of work done

Table 2. Considering constraints

Option	No money available	Workload must be maintained	Staff must feel happy
1.	✓	X	✓
2.	X	✓ after training period	✓
3.	X	✓	?
4.	✓	X	?

impaired by stress. The more pressure you are under, the less able the brain is to use its creative part. Remember, thinking of options is not making a decision or a commitment—that comes later.

Surely this all takes a lot of time?
Yes. But no one is suggesting you waste time unnecessarily. For simple decisions, you might not need to find out any information, you might only have a few options, or you might be able to work out the answer more or less straight away. Use the method in this chapter for longer, more complicated, 'messy' situations, to clarify your ideas and help you justify your decisions.

EVALUATING OPTIONS AND MAKING DECISIONS

Looking at advantages and disadvantages

The simplest way of evaluating the options is to look at the advantages and disadvantages (or pros and cons) of each, and also the likely results of implementing them. For example, using our previous example of how to improve accuracy, the problems were lack of time and low staff motivation. Let's imagine the main options were:

1. reduce workload
2. train staff to work faster and more accurately
3. give incentive or bonus schemes
4. introduce accuracy checks.

Make a chart and fill in the advantages, disadvantages and likely results for each. Table 1 shows this.

From Table 1, we can see that option (2) is obviously likely to produce the best result. However, you do need to check whether you have any *constraints* on your decision. This option will possibly cost money. If none is available, the option can be discounted. It will also take time, and if none can be allowed, again, you need to find another option.

Considering constraints

A further idea is to add columns to the right-hand side of the chart, showing any constraints, and tick or cross to indicate whether they apply to that option. You tick options that are not affected, and cross options that would break the constraint.

An example of this can be seen in Table 2. From this we can see that now, we have no ideal option: option (2) would be best if there was money available, otherwise no option completely solves the problem within the given constraints.

You would have to remove one of the constraints (e.g. allocate some money, or agree to a temporary reduction in workload), or go back and think of some more options. This need not be a problem: one of the main things that people worry about is getting the right answer. Well, there may not be a *right* answer, just a *best* answer.

Your best answer may be a combination of two or more options. In the above example, how about combining options (3) and (4)? Organise a competition among staff for the highest rate of accurate work. This is based on option (3), but involves a competition rather than a bonus or incentive scheme. Monitor accuracy (option (4)), and from the results, award the winner a prize—perhaps a half-day off, or a bottle of wine, or some other incentive that need not cost a great deal. You could award a badge or trophy.

A variation of this would be to use teams of staff in competition with each other. This would have an advantage, as even staff with no chance of winning on an individual basis could still win as part of a team—it motivates everybody.

Can you think of any other possibilities?

Using priorities

If you have difficulty deciding, especially where you have several options that would work, try using some priorities. Let's imagine that all the four options in our example were possible, and all would produce the desired effect. To decide which is the best one, look at what priorities you have, and which order they rank in.

Common priorities would include:

- time
- cost
- equipment
- staff morale/motivation
- meeting targets and deadlines.

Which is the most important? Decide on an order of priority, and see which option is the best, bearing in mind the priorities. This method is very useful when you don't have any constraints to limit your options.

Using weighting

An alternative method is to weight, or score options. You score each option against criteria that are important, which you choose. Score

Table 3. Using weighting

Option	Cost	Time	Staff	Achieving targets	Total
(1)	2	4	2	4	12
(2)	4	2	1	1	8
(3)	3	1	3	2	9
(4)	1	3	4	3	11

one for the best option, and so on. Options which tie are simply given the same score. Add up the points, and the option with the least points wins! Table 3 shows an example of this.

From Table 3, you can see that the best option by far would be option (2), without the constraints we applied earlier. So what would you do, if the lack of available funds really was a constraint? Simply cross the option off the list and don't even consider it in your weighting chart, because it really isn't practical. So only put options which are practical in your weighting chart.

This method is especially good for making open decisions such as buying equipment—which model to buy. Simply list the criteria you would like, then score the options, add up the scores, and see which item best fits your requirements.

An example of using the weighting system to decide which model of computer to purchase is shown in Table 4. Model A is the clear winner, and what is more, you know your decision was *objective*—you weren't persuaded by the salesman's talk, by how the machine looks, or a friend's recommendation—all your judgement was based on was factual criteria. Such judgements and decisions are easy to justify and explain to people, even if the decision is contentious.

IMPLEMENTING, FOLLOWING UP, EVALUATING

So that's it—you've made your decision. But don't stop there: you now need to tie up all the loose ends.

Recording
● Keep a written record of any information gathered, and options

Table 4. Weighting system to decide which computer to purchase

Computer

Model	A	B	C	D	E	F
Easy to use	1	2	3	5	4	6
Long guarantee	2	1	4	3	6	5
Compatible with existing equipment	4	5	2	1	6	3
Reasonable cost	1	6	2	5	4	3
Large memory	1	2	6	3	5	4
Speed of operation	1	4	5	6	2	3
Total	10	20	22	23	27	24

you came up with. If the decision needs to be looked at again, you don't have to 'reinvent the wheel'.

Communicating

- Tell people what you decided, explain why, and let people know how you intend to carry it out. Talking to people face-to-face is best, because you can gauge people's reactions, and 'sell' them the decision if necessary.

- Make sure *everybody* knows—your own boss, other managers and your own staff.

- Ask people how things are going when the decision is in progress. Just because things are working, it doesn't necessarily mean that difficulties are not being experienced.

- If your decision works, thank everyone that helped you with it.

Monitoring and evaluating

- Once the decision is in force, monitor how things go. Check that the expected result actually occurs. If not, you may have to look at the issue again.

- Don't be afraid to make adjustments to your decision if necessary. It doesn't mean you 'got it wrong' if these are necessary, it just means your idea needs refining.

- Check for new problems in other areas that your decision may cause—often changing one thing has a 'knock-on' effect. Again, it doesn't mean your decision is wrong, it just means you now have some other issues to work on.

- If your decision doesn't work, learn from it.

CHECKLIST

- Don't be afraid to ask for help, information, advice or especially ideas.

- Don't put off unpleasant decisions, or when you come to make them, you will be rushed and therefore less able to think creatively.

- Don't keep 'reinventing the wheel'—solving the same problem again and again. If this is happening, you aren't solving it properly!

- Don't be afraid to use intuition. If you have no clear 'best' option, use your intuition—play a 'hunch', follow your 'gut feeling' or 'sixth sense'. These are all names for imaginative, creative thinking.

CASE STUDIES

Bev fails to evaluate options

The care assistants are due to have new uniforms, and Matron asks Bev to choose a design. Bev gets the brochures, and asks everyone what they think. She takes a vote, and puts the first two choices to Matron. The first choice is too expensive, so Matron orders the second choice. When the new uniforms come, they are 'dry clean only', and can't be issued to staff. The exercise has to be done again, and this time Matron chooses. Bev feels very silly. If only she had evaluated the options, and not just picked everyone's favourite.

Nikki needs to be more creative

Nikki is asked to come up with a range of options for producing a new corporate booklet. She gives the job to Peter, who has worked on similar projects in his old job, and Peter decides on a certain format. Nikki goes to her Senior Management Team Meeting and does a short, very polished presentation on the format, but no one likes it. She is sent away to come up with more ideas—several this time, not just one, as she had originally been asked. If only she had involved everybody, she might have got more ideas. She needs to discuss the options and get some creative ideas flowing, to give her a range of options to take forward, rather than just one.

Mike fails to check the quality of information

Mike has a problem tracking down the reason why some figures are not as expected. He asks everyone what they think. Rachel says, 'I don't know. Usually things like this are down to the manager making a mistake.' Tom says, 'Last time it was computer error.' Jo says she will have a look and see what she can come up with, and Sam says, 'I think I can remember someone telephoning and saying something about this. I think the budget manager made a mistake.'

Mike writes a stern memo to the budget manager, asking him to come up with an explanation. The next thing he knows, the man is on the telephone in a flaming temper. Apparently, the computer has put two items together that shouldn't have been there, and he has been unable to undo the error. If only Mike had remembered to check the quality of his information, he could have saved himself a lot of embarrassment.

DISCUSSION POINTS

1. What is the most important decision you have made at work recently? Could the methods in this chapter have helped? Would you have come to the same decision using them?

2. Think of an example where you or someone else made a wrong or bad decision. Apply the methods in this chapter to see what better decision could have been arrived at.

3. Think of a problem you have to solve. What is the real problem? What do you want to achieve—the ideal solution? Now apply the techniques in this chapter to solving it.

Managing Budgets & Cash Flows
How to achieve financial targets in an organisation
Peter Taylor FCA

Second edition

Written by an experienced chartered accountant, this book provides a basic step-by-step introduction to practical budget and cash flow management. It covers planning, forecasting, budgeting, to monitoring performance, both as to current income, and as to capital expenditure on such things as new premises, plant and equipment. The book also covers VAT, costings and margins, and using computers, plus helpful action checklists and short case studies.

£8.99, 160 pp illus. 1 85703 344 2.

Available from How To Books Ltd, Plymbridge House, Estover Road, Plymouth PL6 7PZ.
Customer Services Tel: (01752) 202301. Fax: (01752) 202331.
Please add postage & packing (£1 UK, £2 Europe, £3 world airmail).

Credit card orders may be faxed or phoned.

4
Managing Resources

MANAGING TECHNOLOGY

Technology can be intimidating, but a basic appreciation of what is available and how it works will help you understand how you can make best use of it at work.

Understanding computers

Computers handle masses of data and information at high speed. Three types of computer are common: mainframes, microcomputers and portable computers.

Mainframe
These have a huge information processing capacity, and are large systems which are used via a **terminal**. A terminal is simply a screen (called a visual display unit—a VDU—or monitor) and a keyboard, connected electronically to the mainframe, or central computer. The mainframe itself can be many miles away, and usually needs an air-conditioned room to protect it from things like dirt, dust and humidity.

Microcomputers
These are often called personal computers or PCs. They are smaller, and consist of a screen and keyboard, the computer processor itself, and usually a disc drive for recording and reading information on computer discs.

Portable computers
These are often called laptops or notebooks, because they are so small. They have the features and capabilities of PCs in a portable form.

Networking
Computers are often linked electronically to form a network. This

means that the linked computers can communicate electronically with each other. The advantage of this is that information can be accessed by any computer in the network.

Modems
A modem connects a computer to others through the telephone system. This allows you to transmit and receive information. While the modem is connected, you are part of the network, but the connection is broken when the modem is disconnected. The **Internet,** an international information network, may be accessed by modem, and many people use this to access information.

Scanners
Scanners read printed or drawn material from a page into a computer. With them, you can input pictures, maps, diagrams etc into the computer.

E-mail
E-mail is electronic mail. It is simply sending and receiving electronic information over a network or modem, rather than on paper.

Appreciating modern telecommunications
Telephones have been in use for very many years. Technology is changing our telecommunications, however, with new improved devices and systems, to save time and make life easier.

Voice-mail
Voice-mail systems use a computer as well as a telephone system. They are similar to an answerphone, taking messages, but can do much more, giving you far more options. They are usually operated by pressing code keys on your telephone, and so you need a 'tone phone' to use them. This is a telephone that 'beeps' when you press the keys—the sound tells the computer what to do, just like pressing a key on a computer keyboard. Voice-mail systems are already in use for telephone banking and for queuing systems, and more applications are being developed all the time.

Call forwarding
This means you can programme your phone to automatically forward all your calls to another phone.

Conference calls
The operator can connect several people to the same telephone

conversation. This allows several people to take part in a conversation at once.

It is worth asking your operator what facilities you can use on your telephone, as they will be able to keep you up-to-date with all the latest developments.

MANAGING STOCK

Stock can mean many things. We often talk about **consumables**, which are materials and supplies which are frequently used and therefore need replacing often, such as paper, pens, envelopes, scissors etc.

Stock can also mean warehouse goods. Non-consumable items are usually called **capital items**, as this sort of stock forms part of the capital or worth of the organisation.

Stock control

Good stock control keeps costs down, while keeping enough stock available. It involves receiving stock, storing and checking (auditing) it, ordering it, and issuing it. Some organisations have manual systems to keep track of stock, while others use a computer system.

It does not matter whether you are dealing with a warehouse full of capital items or a cupboard full of stationery—the principles of good stock control are the same.

Fig. 11 shows the stock cycle.

Receiving stock

Check goods received carefully for damaged, incomplete or missing items. Do not rely on delivery notes—unpack goods, count and check them yourself. If there are any problems, inform the supplier immediately. You can also take the following steps.

Damaged items
Check before you sign for the items whether you are signing to say they are in good condition. If so, do not sign, or write the details of the damage on the delivery note before signing it.

Missing items
Check the delivery note for items marked 'out of stock', 'to follow' or 'discontinued'. 'Out of stock' means there are no supplies, and you need to reorder. 'To follow' means they will be sent separately later (keep a note of this and check they do arrive). 'Discontinued' means the item is no longer available. Some suppliers automatically send a

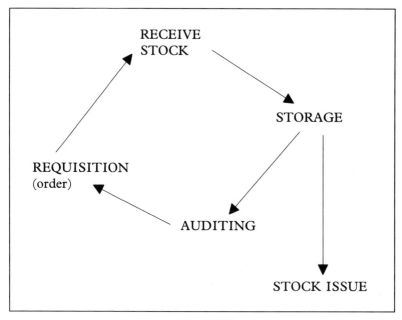

Fig. 11. The stock cycle.

replacement for these, but legally you do not have to accept replacement items if they are not suitable. Do not sign for the items unless the discrepancies are clearly shown on the delivery note.

Incorrect or additional items
These goods should be returned. Ensure your organisation does not pay for them.

Storing stock

● Guard against theft.

● Keep a proper record of exactly what stock you have.

● Keep faster moving items where they are most easily accessible.

● Keep large bulky items low down to avoid heavy lifting.

● Know which items are *active* and which are *inactive*. Active items are frequently used and need a high level of stock available. Inactive items are less frequently used, and need only a low level of stock.

- Label all stock clearly.

- Store hazardous items safely and legally.

- Store stock carefully to prevent waste and damage.

- Store stock with labels facing upwards and outwards, so they can easily be read.

- Undertake regular checks to see if stocks of any item are running low.

- Use stock in rotation, so items do not get left in stock for long periods of time. Rotation means always issuing your oldest stock and keeping the newest. This ensures your stock does not get outdated. Place new stock under or behind old stock to ensure this.

Auditing stock

- Carry out a regular stock check or stock inventory, by counting stock against the recorded levels.

- Investigate any discrepancies carefully.

- Adjust the stock record to take account of any unusable stock, so it can be disposed of. Examples of this would be stock damaged beyond use, or stock which is obsolete, or out of date.

Issuing stock

- Only issue stock to authorised people.

- Monitor excessive requests for stock or short-notice urgent demands—perhaps these could be avoided by better planning.

Ordering stock

- Order stock in good time—remembering there will probably be a delivery time. Stock does not magically appear as soon as you order it.

- When you order stock, remember you will probably have used up some more of the item before the new delivery arrives. You might therefore want to order more than required, to compensate for this.

- Be aware of any maximum stock levels set. These are important, as holding stock ties up money (working capital) which might be needed elsewhere in the organisation.

QUESTIONS AND ANSWERS

We have computers and word processors at work, but I've never used one. Does it matter?
Not unless you need to use one for your job. However, they are nothing to be afraid of. Most adult education centres do evening classes in computing, and you could learn more that way. At work, it would be useful if you made sure you were aware of what the computers do—what information they handle and what jobs they do. You can't make effective use of them as a resource unless you understand their capabilities.

We regularly run out of some items. Where am I going wrong?
In one of two ways. Perhaps you don't keep enough of these items in stock, so you need to order larger quantities and stock up. Alternatively, perhaps you are ordering enough, but because it takes a long time for the new stock to be delivered, you run out before the new supply arrives. If this is the case, order earlier—set a level, and as soon as stock gets down to that level, reorder. Once you have found the right level you should have no more problems.

MANAGING MONEY—PETTY CASH AND INVOICES

Petty cash
Petty cash is money kept to cover small items of day-to-day expenditure. The amount held varies, depending on how long the money is supposed to last—normally one week or one month. The amount held may sometimes be called an **imprest account.**

Why use cash?
- For emergency purchases, e.g. special postage.

- To pay people who only accept cash, e.g. the milkman, or office window cleaner.

- To pay for purchases too small to warrant an invoice or cheque.

Checking petty cash

- Check that expenditure is only for authorised payments.

- Check that expenditure is recorded accurately and substantiated by a receipt or voucher.

- Check the cash is secure at all times.

- Check that the amount held is exactly the amount that should be left, after deducting receipts and vouchers.

Using vouchers and receipts

Some organisations pay people from petty cash in return for a receipt. Other organisations use petty cash vouchers—these are an authority to spend money, and should ideally have a receipt attached. You need receipts or vouchers to balance the petty cash—simply add up amounts on the receipts and vouchers paid, and this is the total paid out. Subtract this from the petty cash total, and the remainder should be what you have in cash.

Replacing petty cash

When the petty cash runs low, it needs to be replaced by Accounts or the appropriate person. You add up the expenditure in categories, and total how much has been spent. This can then be replaced, so you have a full amount of petty cash again.

If the petty cash runs out before the end of the week or month regularly, consider asking for an increase in the amount held. This will save you time and work.

Checking invoices and invoice terms

The following is a list of things you may see on an invoice, and gives some advise on how to check them.

Carrier forward

This means the buyer is liable to pay the delivery charges.

Carriage paid

This means the supplier will pay the delivery charges. Check that delivery charges do not get added to the invoice.

Cash discount

This is a discount given for prompt payment. Terms should be quoted on the invoice. Check the discount is deducted and is the right amount.

Credit note

This is a note sent because a previous invoice charged too much. This may be because goods were overcharged, goods were returned, or fewer goods were delivered than on the invoice. If you are expecting a credit note, you must monitor carefully that it arrives and that it is for the correct amount.

Debit note

This is a supplementary invoice. It means that the original invoice did not include all the charges. It is usually because goods were undercharged, too many goods were sent, more expensive goods were sent, or an item was omitted from the original invoice. Check these invoices carefully to be sure the charges have not been previously paid.

Delivery address

Check it is the right address.

Delivery charges

Check that you should be paying these and not the supplier. Check that they are at the correct rate.

Description/reference number

Check that the item(s) are what was ordered.

Discount

Check that the rate of discount quoted is correct and that the discount has been calculated correctly.

Dispatch date

Check the goods have been dispatched, i.e. check that the date is in the past. Check against a delivery note or goods received note that they have been received.

Errors and omissions excepted

Invoices often say 'E&OE', which mean errors and omissions excepted. This means that if there are any items missed off, or any mistakes have been made, the supplier retains the right to send you a supplementary invoice.

Name

Check the invoice carries your name and/or the right organisation's name. Otherwise, it may cause accounting or auditing problems.

Order number

Check against the order that the order bears the correct number—this means the order was authorised and ordered officially.

Price

Check the order or the quotation to ensure the price is correct.

Quantity

Check that the quantity quoted is both what was ordered and what was received.

Statement

This is a statement of the account, and should list all invoices, payments made and credits, and an overall balance. They are usually issued monthly, like a bank statement. They need to be carefully checked.

Supplementary invoices

These are also called debit notes (see above).

Terms for payment

Check that these are as agreed, and that you are paying within the agreed time.

Total price

Check the calculations have been added up correctly.

Trade discount

This is a discount given as an allowance if large orders are placed, or if the supplier is in the same trade as your organisation. Check that the discount is deducted.

VAT rate

Check that the VAT rate is correct, and that the amount of VAT has been calculated correctly.

CHECKLIST

- Find out what technology is available in your workplace, and what it can do.

- Keep careful stock control—audit regularly, and keep good records.

- Be alert for discrepancies when receiving stock.

- Store stock well, so it is safe, secure and easy to handle.

- Order stock carefully, and check all invoices, delivery notes and other paperwork.

- Always keep accurate accounts of petty cash.

CASE STUDIES

Bev's assistant fails to check a delivery

When the new staff uniforms come, it is late in the day, and Bev is busy. A new girl, Lucy, signs for them so the delivery man can get away. When they are unpacked, there are two uniforms less than on the delivery note. Bev tells Matron, who telephones the company at once, but the company says that the correct number have been sent. Lucy gets into trouble because she isn't authorised to sign for the delivery, and should have got Bev. Bev always checks deliveries carefully, and had she been called, the situation could have been avoided.

Nikki learns about stock security

Nikki doesn't bother keeping the office stationery locked away. 'People need to be able to get things as and when they need them—this is a busy office,' she was told when she took over. After five months, she orders some more notebooks and computer discs from stores, but is told that her consumables allocation has all been spent. She needs paper and discs, and has to go and see her manager about it. Obviously, somebody is dishonest, but who? A lot of people have access to the office, including when Nikki and her team have gone home. Nikki learns the hard way to keep stock safe and secure, and monitor it at all times.

Mike investigates the petty cash

Mike's section runs the department coffee bar. They use petty cash for purchases, and have an imprest account of £100 per month to do this. Mike lets Tom look after this, as he has been doing it since before Mike arrived. After a while, he notices that Tom regularly asks for a 'top-up'—more petty cash in the middle of the month. On investigation, Mike finds that other sections all come to Tom for petty cash, for all sorts of things—taxis, parking tickets, emergency stationery supplies—anything. This means that Tom has been spending a lot of his time running a petty cash account for other sections. Mike also realises that Tom could be in trouble—he is not authorised to issue petty cash for those purposes. If only Mike had checked Tom's accounts more carefully.

DISCUSSION POINTS

1. What stock do you control? Is it properly recorded and accounted for? How could you improve your stock handling?

2. Do you check invoices correctly? What procedures do you have for making sure that errors are corrected and accounted for?

5
Managing Standards

As managers, we have certain legal obligations. The law gives employees rights, and places obligations and responsibilities on employers and managers. This chapter is intended to give you an insight into three main areas of your legal responsibility—health and safety, data protection and employment law.

MANAGING HEALTH AND SAFETY AT WORK

Health and safety at work is everyone's responsibility. However, as a manager, you can be held personally responsible for health and safety—responsible for ensuring that your organisation operates safely and with due regard for health. You have a second responsibility to do whatever is reasonably practicable to achieve this.

Understanding the Health and Safety at Work Act 1974

This piece of legislation is called an **enabling** act. This means it is general in nature and covers a broad range of situations and issues. It is an Act through which further legislation can be (and already has been) added. The Act had four main aims:

- To ensure the health, safety and welfare of people at work, by giving responsibility for it to everybody—employees, supervisors and managers.

- To protect non-employees from risks to their health or safety which might come from employees and their work.

- To control storage and use of explosive, flammable or dangerous substances, and to prevent such substances being obtained, possessed or used unless a person is legally entitled to do so.

- To control emissions of noxious or poisonous substances into the atmosphere.

What did the Act do?

- It brought the law on health, safety and welfare at work up-to-date.

- It created a Health and Safety Commission, which has inspectors to give advice and to enforce the regulations.

- It created a range of duties which employers had to carry out.

- It reorganised the various existing government inspectors.

- It gave new powers and penalties to enforce safety laws.

- It established new accident prevention measures.

- It established **Codes of Practice** instead of regulations. The advantage of these is that they are written in non-legal language which can be more easily understood, and they can be revised easily to keep up with new developments and technology. The Codes can be used as evidence in court, to show what good safe practice is.

Knowing your responsibilities under the Act

The Act details a number of duties which apply to employers, employees and non-employees. These duties are important to us as managers, as we need to carry them out to comply with the law. As managers, we are employers under the Act, although we are also employees—so we have twice as many duties as non-managers!

Understanding the duties of employers to employees

Section 2 of the Act covers the duties of employers to employees. The main duties are as follows:

- You have a duty to ensure so far as is reasonably practicable, the health, safety and welfare at work of employees.

- You have a duty to provide and maintain **plant** (machinery, equipment and appliances used at work) that is safe and without health risks.

- You have a duty to ensure that everything used at work and all work activities are safe and without health risk. This especially refers to handling, transport and storage of materials and substances.

- You have a duty to provide information, instruction, training and supervision, so employees are safe and without health risk at work.

- You have a duty to maintain any place of work under your control in a safe and health-risk-free condition. You also have a duty to provide facilities, entrances, exits and arrangements for welfare at work that are safe and free from health risk.

- You have a duty to prepare and revise a written health and safety policy statement. You also have a duty to bring this to the attention of all employees.

Understanding the duties of employers to non-employees

- You have a responsibility to protect non-employees, such as members of the public at your place of work.

- You have a duty to carry out business in such a way that non-employees who may be affected by the business are not exposed to risks to their health or safety.

- You have a duty to give non-employees information about things that may affect their health or safety.

Understanding the other duties of employers

As an employer, you also have certain special duties. These apply:

- if you are in charge of any premises;

- if you *design* any article, plant, machinery, equipment or appliance for use at work;

- if you *manufacture* any article, plant, machinery, equipment or appliance for use at work;

- if you *import* any article, plant, machinery, equipment or appliance for use at work;

- if you *supply* any article, plant, machinery, equipment or appliance for use at work;

- if you *erect* any article, plant, machinery, equipment or appliance for use at work;

- if you *install* any article, plant, machinery, equipment or appliance for use at work;

- if you *manufacture* any substance for use at work;

- if you *import* any substance for use at work;

- if you *supply* any substance for use at work.

Understanding the duties of employees

All employees, including managers, have three main duties:

- You have a duty to take reasonable care of your own health and safety, and that of others who may be affected by the things you do or do not do at work.

- You have a duty to co-operate with your employer as far as necessary, to enable them to carry out their own duties and requirements.

- You have a duty not to intentionally or recklessly misuse or interfere with anything provided for health, safety or welfare purposes.

What happens when things go wrong?

Inspectors

Inspectors have the power to enter any premises at any reasonable time. They have the power to bring an authorised person with them, and to take samples, measurements, photographs and recordings. They have the power to require people to provide information, to answer questions, and to sign a declaration of truth.

When an inspector feels that health and safety needs enforcing, they have the power to do two things:

1. *Improvement notices*—an organisation is 'served with' (given) an improvement notice if an inspector thinks that the law has been contravened. An improvement notice gives the details, and asks the employer to put the situation right within a specified amount of time.

2. *Prohibition notices*—an organisation is served with a prohibition notice if an inspector thinks there is a risk of serious personal injury. A prohibition notice means that work must stop immediately. If the inspector thinks the risk is not imminent, they may issue a **deferred** prohibition notice. This means that work must stop if matters are not put right within a certain period of time.

Penalties

If you do not comply with an improvement notice, a prohibition notice or a deferred prohibition notice, you may be taken to court and fined or imprisoned.

The Management of Health and Safety at Work Regulations 1992

These Regulations came into force on 1 January 1993, under the provisions of the Health & Safety at Work Act 1974. They were produced to enable the UK to implement a European Community directive made under the Treaty of Rome. This directive called upon all member states of the European Community to:

- encourage health and safety
- manage health and safety
- improve attitudes towards health and safety.

The Regulations are in addition to the Health and Safety at Work Act 1974. They extend the employer's general safety obligations by requiring additional specific actions to enhance control measures for health and safety.

The ten main requirements of the Regulations are as follows:

- Making arrangements for health surveillance.

- Setting out formal management control systems (effective monitoring, control and review).

- The appointment of a competent person (appointed by the employer) to assist in compliance with the obligations under legislation, and ideally a safety officer.

- To carry out capability assessments (to assess the competency of the workforce).

- To carry out risk assessment (assessments of risk by the employer and the self-employed).

- To encourage inter-employer co-operation ('Sharing the work-place').

- To lay down procedures for serious and imminent danger (fire drills etc).

- To provide information for workers (upon starting and job changes).

- To provide job-specific training (induction, and for use of new equipment).

- For employees to report hazards.

Checklist of good practice for managers

☐ Allocate responsibility to people for health and safety.

☐ Carry out a regular inspection of the workplace, looking for hazards and risks.

☐ Check adequate first aid facilities are available.

☐ Check safe working practices and methods are in use.

☐ Ensure employees are trained in health and safety.

☐ Ensure all health and safety measures under your responsibility are carried out.

☐ Give employees a written health and safety policy.

☐ Carry out induction for new employees, so they know about health and safety.

☐ Issue and regularly check safety equipment and protective cloth-ing. Also ensure that this is used or worn whenever necessary.

☐ Liaise with superiors about health and safety.

☐ Make sure that you have proper procedures for working that are safe, to prevent accidents. These should be in writing if possible.

☐ Provide appropriate fire-fighting equipment, and make sure that fire drills are carried out regularly.

☐ Remind employees regularly about health and safety.

☐ Report all accidents, near-misses and hazards.

☐ Set up a safety group or committee, or make sure employees know how to make suggestions and bring things to your attention about health and safety.

☐ Carry out regular assessments of risks.

Reporting injuries, diseases and dangerous occurrences regulations (RIDDOR)

The Reporting of Injuries, Diseases and Dangerous Occurrences Regulations 1985 require you to report certain incidents to the Health and Safety Executive, or to the environmental health department of your local authority. Failing to do this is a criminal offence. The Regulations were made so that trends in incidents could be seen on a national basis, and advice given as to how to avoid common incidents.

What to report
You must immediately report, by telephone:

● any fatal or major injuries to anybody in an accident connected with your business

● any dangerous occurrences listed in the Regulations.

You must also report in writing and within seven days:

● any of the above

● any other injury to an employee which results in them being away from work or unable to do their normal work for more than three days (including weekends and days off)

● any cases of ill health listed in the Regulations.

Record-keeping
You must keep a record of anything you need to report. This record must include the date, time, place, personal details and a brief description of the event.

PROTECTING COMPUTER DATA

Information is held about everybody on computer—from the day we are born, computers collect and store information about us and our identity. Computer records have many advantages—they are faster and more efficient than looking up information manually. However, there are potential problems to having information stored about you on a computer, and the Data Protection Act 1984 was introduced to set standards for accuracy and use of computer data.

What does the Act cover?
The Act only covers information that is:

- automatically processed (which usually means processed by computer)

- about living, identifiable individuals (including children).

How does the Act work?
The Act gives rights to individuals, and sets responsibilities for data users.

Individual rights
- You have the right as an individual to see information about you which is held on a computer.

- You have the right as an individual to complain about the misuse of your information.

- You have the right as an individual to go to court to seek compensation if you suffer damage from inaccurate data, from unauthorised destruction of your data, or from unauthorised disclosure of your data.

Responsibilities for data users
- Users of personal data have to register with the Data Protection Registrar.

- Users of personal data have to follow **principles** (rules) when collecting or using personal information.

Exceptions to the Act

There are three exceptions to the Act, where people or organisations do not have to register or follow the principles. These are:

- if the data is held by an individual for domestic or recreational purposes, e.g. personal address lists or lists of birthdays

- if the data is being held purely for payroll, pensions or accounts

- if the data is being used to provide a simple mailing list.

How do you register?

To register, simply fill in a registration form. These are available from the Registrar's office, and have notes to help you. There is a fee to cover registration for a certain period of time.

QUESTIONS AND ANSWERS

This all sounds very technical and complicated. Where can I get more information?

Further information about health and safety, including a wide range of leaflets, can be obtained from:

The Health and Safety Executive Information Centre
Broad Lane
Sheffield
S3 7HQ

For further information about data protection, contact:

The Office of the Data Protection Registrar
Wycliffe House
Water Lane
Wilmslow
Cheshire
SK9 5AF

What are the consequences if I don't carry out all my duties?

Ultimately, you may end up in court—not to obey the Health and

Safety at Work Act or the Data Protection Act is committing a criminal offence. You can be prosecuted, and fined in court, or even imprisoned.

UNDERSTANDING EMPLOYMENT LAW

The law gives employees certain rights. These **statutory rights** apply to part-time as well as full-time workers, but do not apply to people working for an organisation on a self-employed basis (apart from health and safety legislation). **Homeworkers** (people working from home) may be employees, or self-employed. If they are employees, they are covered by statutory law.

As an employer, you must observe the statutory rights of employees, or you are in breach of the law, and you can be penalised. The main way of doing this is by an **industrial tribunal**. If an employer wishes, they can be more generous than the minimum statutory requirements. If this happens, the better rights are usually written into the employee's contract. An employer cannot put things into a contract which are *less* beneficial than the employee's statutory rights.

Some of the rights have a **qualifying period** or minimum period of time an employee has to have worked to be entitled to them. Some rights list **exemptions**—categories of employee who are not covered by them. In this chapter, you will find the rights listed, but this does not mean that they apply to everybody—some people will be exempt or will not have worked the minimum qualifying period. *You will need to check the relevant legislation in detail to find out all the exact qualifying periods and exemptions.*

Pay

- Employees have the right to pay when they would normally expect to work but no work is available. This means if people are laid off for a whole day or days, they have the right to pay.

- Employees have the right to an itemised statement of pay at the time of payment. This must detail gross earnings, net pay and fixed and variable deductions.

- If their employer becomes insolvent, an employee has the right to wages and other payment rights as if they were wages payable under the Bankruptcy Acts and Companies Acts.

- Employees have the right to information about their occupational pension schemes.

Maternity
- Pregnant employees have the right to maternity leave, and the right to return to their old job after giving birth.

- Women have the right not to be required to return to work (including sending work home to them) within two weeks of giving birth. For women working in factories, this period of time is four weeks.

- Women have the right to maternity pay.

- Women have the right to a written reason for dismissal, if dismissed whilst pregnant or on maternity leave.

- Pregnant women have the right to paid time off for ante-natal care.

Periods of notice
- Employees have the right to notice after one month's service.

- Employees who are given notice have the right to be paid during the notice period, regardless of whether or not they are able to work.

Sickness
- Employees have the right to full pay if they are suspended from work on medical grounds for certain conditions.

- Employees have the right to Statutory Sick Pay for absences of four days or more.

- Employees have the right to withhold consent, so the employer cannot insist on a medical report from an employee's own doctor.

- Employees have the right to have access to any medical report, before it goes to their employer. They also have the right to comment on that report, or to refuse consent to it being passed to their employer, or to request incorrect or misleading parts of the report to be corrected.

Time off
- Employees have the right to have time off (unpaid) to fulfil duties as a:
  —justice of the peace
  —local councillor
  —member of a statutory tribunal
  —member of a regional or area health authority
  —governor or manager of a state school
  —member of the National Rivers Authority
  —member of Boards of Visitors in England, Wales or Scotland
  —member of Visiting Committees to prisons, remand centres and young offender institutions.

- Employees who are made redundant have the right to reasonable paid time off to look for a new job, or to arrange training for a new job.

- Employees have the right to take unpaid leave to carry out reserve military duties.

- Employees who are called up to military service have the right to return to employment afterwards.

Health and safety
- Employees have the right to a healthy and safe working environment.

- Members of recognised trade unions have the right to ask the company to set up a safety committee, on which they may be represented.

Trade unions
- Employees have the right to belong to an independent trade union of their choice.

- Employees have the right to refuse to belong to a staff association that is not independent (i.e. one that is subject to interference by the company).

Infringement of rights
- Employees dismissed for trying to obtain their statutory rights have the right to complain to an industrial tribunal.

The main Acts and Regulations relevant in employment law
Access to Medical Reports Act 1988
Access to Medical Records Act 1990
Companies Act 1985
Data Protection Act 1984
Employment Act 1980
Employment Act 1988
Employment Act 1989
Employment Act 1990
Employment Protection (Consolidation) Act 1978
Employment Protection (Part-Time) Employees Regulations 1995
Factories Act 1961
Health and Safety at Work Act 1974
Maternity (Compulsory Leave) Regulations 1994
Offices, Shops and Railway Premises Act
Reserve Forces (Safeguard of Employment) Act 1985
Sex Discrimination Act 1975
Sex Discrimination Act 1986
Social Services Contributions and Benefits Act 1992
Trade Union and Labour Relations (Consolidation) Act 1992
Trade Union Reform and Employment Rights Act 1993
Wages Act 1986

CHECKLIST

- Be aware of your responsibilities for health and safety, data protection and employment law.

- Know what your organisation's policies and procedures are regarding these three areas.

- Query anything which you are not sure about.

- Get specialist advice or information in the relevant legislation whenever necessary.

CASE STUDIES

Bev fails to prevent an accident
Bev notices a piece of carpet which has frayed. She makes a mental note to put up a sign. However, with everything else she has on that day, she forgets. When she goes into work the next day, she is going

along the corridor with Sheila, one of the care assistants, when Sheila trips. She caught her toe under the frayed carpet. 'Sorry Sheila!' Bev exclaims. 'I meant to put a notice up—I'll do it right away.' So, she goes and puts a notice on the wall by the frayed section. That evening, one of the care assistants from the night shift catches her foot in the carpet and trips, spilling hot coffee over another girl. The notice has fallen down. Bev feels very guilty, and blames herself.

Matron blames Bev too. 'Why didn't you put this in the accident book?' she asks. 'But there wasn't an accident!' Bev replies. If only she had remembered that by reporting near-misses and incidents which happen, actual accidents can often be avoided.

Nikki omits to follow Data Protection rules

Nikki's predecessor left a file on the computer, containing the details of all the staff in the office and records of their performance. This file was shown to Nikki when she arrived, and as Nikki's personal password was needed to get into the file, no one else could access the information. Nikki finds it useful to record performance details each week, to remind her at appraisal time how staff have done, and to keep a record of any problems. One day, whilst tidying up some computer files and deleting old information, Peter finds the file, but can't read it. 'What's this file?' he asks Nikki. 'It says "Staff Records".' Nikki explains what it is. Peter is very offended that records about him are kept on the computer.

As Nikki is explaining, the Administration Manager walks in. He is not pleased. The file has never been registered for Data Protection purposes, and contains confidential information on addresses, date of birth etc. If only Nikki had checked at regular intervals that her Data Protection registration was up-to-date.

Mike learns about maternity rights

Rachel tells Mike she is expecting a baby. After a few months, she begins to phone in sick in the mornings, with morning sickness. As she is often late coming into the office, her work begins to pile up. Then she comes to Mike and asks for time off for ante-natal classes. 'What?' Mike explodes. 'Rachel, you're hardly here as it is! You're a good worker, but your work's so far behind we can't cope with it all. You'll have to make up the time. I don't mind you going, it's your right, but you'll need either to take work home or stay late to cover the time.'

Rachel complains to Personnel, and the Personnel Officer asks Mike to come and speak to him. 'If only you'd asked me first, I would have told you you can't do this,' he says. 'Pregnant employees have the right to time off for ante-natal classes. It's the law.' Mike should have asked for advice before saying anything to the employee.

DISCUSSION POINTS

1. Do you have a copy of your organisation's health and safety policy? Do all your staff know about it? Are they trained to work safely in everything they do?

2. What data do you hold on computer? Is it registered with the Data Protection Registrar? If not, does it need to be?

3. Do you know where to get advice on employment issues, for example from Personnel? Do you know what your responsibilities for staff are?

6
Managing Meetings

MAKING MEETINGS SUCCESSFUL

Meetings can be a nightmare. However, there is a formula for successful meetings, and following it should guarantee you better meetings, whether you are running them (called 'chairing' them) or just attending. One of the keys lies in knowing that there are two results you want from a meeting—satisfaction and achievement of business.

A meeting can be successful in achieving its business, but if that is done in a way that leaves those present feeling dissatisfied, they are less likely to co-operate next time. Conversely, an enjoyable meeting is not necessarily successful, unless it also achieves its business.

The formula for a successful meeting can be found in Fig. 12.

SETTING AGENDAS

The **agenda** is a list of what is to be dealt with at a meeting. It need not be a formal document—it simply needs to state:

- where and when the meeting will take place
- who is expected to attend
- a list of items to be discussed (**agenda items**).

It is usual that the first item on the agenda is approval of the notes of the last meeting (called **minutes**), and the last items are 'Any Other Business' and the date of the next meeting. 'Any Other Business' allows discussion of items that weren't on the agenda.

The most important thing about an agenda is that it goes to people who are expected to attend early enough, so they have time to prepare for the meeting if necessary. An agenda needs to be both realistic and purposeful.

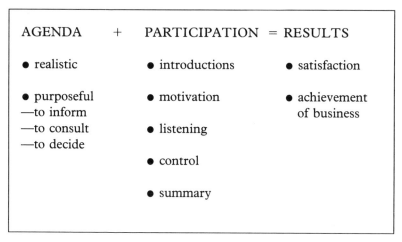

AGENDA   +   PARTICIPATION   = RESULTS

● realistic   ● introductions   ● satisfaction

● purposeful   ● motivation   ● achievement
—to inform   of business
—to consult   ● listening
—to decide
                     ● control

                     ● summary

Fig. 12. Formula for a successful meeting.

Be realistic

Agendas need to be realistic. This means they need to be achievable within the time allowed—not too long.

Give purpose

Make agendas purposeful. This means letting people know the purpose of items, so they know what to expect. An item can be on an agenda for one of three reasons:

● to inform
● to consult
● to reach a decision.

Make sure members of meetings know *why* the item is on the agenda. For example, don't let people think they are going to discuss and decide on something, if the item is only there to inform them of what has already been agreed elsewhere.

Do your homework

● Has this item arisen before?

● If so, what happened then?

● Try to find out who supports and who opposes an item.

- Have an agreed fallback position—a compromise you can resort to if things are going badly.

Beware of timing

How do you allocate time to each item? Most people don't bother, which is why so many meetings take so long! If you allocate time, you have much more chance of achieving your business.

- Agree in advance a time limit for each item. This will prevent meetings overrunning. You don't have to put a time limit on the agenda, you can set one in your own mind.

- Consider how important an item is. Allow more time for more important items.

- Consider the likely desire of people to speak on a subject. You may need to allow extra time for people to make their points on a contentious subject, even if it is a relatively minor item, to 'clear the air'.

- Don't confuse important items with urgent items. Remember importance and urgency (see Chapter 2)? Urgent items deserve a quick mention, but may not necessarily require much time.

Issue documentation

- Consider when to issue papers or documents in advance. Do you need opinions, reactions, decisions on the day? If so, would it help if people had relevant information in advance to read?

- Is there too much to take in during the day? If so, could some things be sent out in advance?

- *Can* the information be circulated in advance, or does it really need verbal explanation to avoid confusion?

GAINING PARTICIPATION

The five factors in achieving participation are:

- introductions
- motivation
- listening
- control
- summary.

The same principles apply, whether you are chairing or just attending a meeting—you can do all these things as an 'attendee' to help yourself and others participate effectively. However, let's assume you are 'in the chair' yourself.

Give introductions

- Introduce members on arrival. Introduce self as chairperson. Who feels strongly about which subjects? Does anyone have to leave early? If so, would it be helpful to rearrange the sequence of the agenda?

- Introduce new members. Introduce visitors, and arrange to deal with their agenda item as soon as possible.

- Introduce each item on the agenda concisely. Refer to past history where appropriate. Give clear indications of the purpose of the item on the agenda: to inform, consult or decide.

Give motivation

- Always remember that to encourage input, you may have to put someone on the spot.

- Be aware of specialist interests among those present.

- Bring in quiet members. Canvas opinions. Be open about needing input due to your own lack of detailed knowledge.

- Encourage contributions from members.

- To start debate, call on different viewpoints alternately. You must be seen to be balanced and give justice to all.

Listening

- Listening is an active behaviour—you need to be *seen* to be listening! Use nods, looks, eye contact, questions to clarify understanding.

- Always try to see and understand the other point of view.

- Listen to the minority.

Controlling

- Always remember that, above all else, people expect that the chairperson will do something to control the meeting.

- Control by choosing and using allies and enemies.

- Control by formality (formal procedures), timing (pacing the meeting and allocating timings) or behaviour.

- Control contributions, especially proposals, and keep track of debate direction. Steer discussions if necessary. Too light control means discussions wander; too heavy and you risk appearing to have your mind already made up.

- Control through courtesy.

- Do not let 'multiple meetings' start—they are distracting.

- Know when to give in, to preserve the integrity of your status as chairperson.

Summarising

- Give periodic summaries. Highlight key points and review progress.

- Give general summaries in technical discussions, to ensure understanding.

- Summarise at the meeting's end. This is a second chance to 'smooth any ruffled feathers', thank people for contributions, and remind members of agreed actions/tasks/responsibilities.

Holding pre-meetings

You can gain a preview of what may occur in a difficult, important meeting by having a pre-meeting, with only a few people rather than the full meeting.

Advantages
- They let you test opinions.
- You can iron out problems.
- You can 'strike deals'.

Disadvantages
● The meeting itself might appear a 'fait accompli'.
● You might get lulled into a false sense of security.
● You could alienate some people, by appearing to exclude them.

QUESTIONS AND ANSWERS

So are good meetings down to the chairperson then?
Usually. The best chairperson in the world won't stop some people, if they are determined to be difficult. But in most instances, a good chairperson can make a huge difference. In meetings where you are not chairing, don't rely on the chairperson—remember all the points on the previous pages, and put them into practice, and it will help enormously.

Do we have to have a chairperson?
No. This is too formal for some meetings. However, most meetings without a chairperson will find that someone 'takes over' and controls things—people have a natural tendency to expect someone to take charge. In many meetings, one person is more senior than the others, and people may naturally assume that those people will run the meeting.

What about motions and proposals and things?
If you ever attend any formal meetings where these are used, you will need to look up exactly what procedures and rules apply. However, for most people, these are formalities they will never need to know about.

TAKING MINUTES

Notes of a meeting are called **minutes**. In a formal meeting, a chairperson and secretary may be appointed. The secretary's job is to send out the agenda and other papers, and to take the minutes. In other meetings of a less formal nature, a volunteer may take the minutes down on paper, or the chairperson him/herself may do this.

Who should take them?

It is not necessarily a good idea to take your own minutes if you are in charge of a meeting. The advantage is that you control what is written down. The disadvantage, however, is that you have to control the meeting, listen, understand and participate, and write notes all at once. A better idea is to get someone else to do the minutes for you.

How to format them

The format of minutes varies—some organisations have a set format, in others you are free to produce them in your own way. However they are laid out, minutes usually take a certain sequence. A typical sequence is given below.

1. *Description*: A sentence saying what the meeting was, where and when it was held.

2. *Presence*: A list of people present, and a list of people unable to attend (called **apologies**).

3. *Minutes of the last meeting*: A statement saying whether everyone agreed that the minutes of the last meeting were reasonably accurate, and detailing any discussions about them (called **matters arising**).

4. *Agenda items*: Notes on each item discussed in the same order as they appeared on the agenda. Details of any discussions made. Details of any action to be taken *must* be recorded. Include the name of who is to take action, so people know what they have to do.

5. *Any other business*: Anything discussed that was not on the agenda, recorded as for agenda items.

6. *Date of the next meeting*: The date of the next meeting is given.

Distributing minutes

It is usual to give everyone (including those who didn't attend) a copy of the minutes. Some people do this before the next meeting. Others prefer to send the minutes with the agenda for the next meeting, or even to give them out at the beginning of the next meeting.

CHECKLIST

- Always keep your cool. Remember—control through courtesy.

- Be prepared for the worst, and even if it happens, you will be able to cope.

- Prepare in advance.

- Don't take things personally. Remember, you are discussing an item, not you and your management.

- Don't let discussions get personal.

- Don't be over-organised—be flexible enough to allow and encourage participation.

CASE STUDIES

Bev's staff meeting runs out of time

Bev holds a staff meeting with all her shift members. She has a number of items she needs to discuss, and writes out a list of these as an informal agenda. She takes this to the meeting so she doesn't forget anything. People want to discuss some things in more detail than Bev has anticipated, and Bev has difficulty controlling things. In the end, some items are discussed in great depth, with a lot of unnecessary detail. Others near the end of Bev's list don't get discussed at all, as they run out of time. If only Bev had given a copy of the agenda to everyone, they would have realised how much there was to be discussed, and they might well have stuck to the points in hand.

Nikki produces the wrong figures

Nikki goes to the monthly management meeting. One item is 'Sales Receipts', and when Nikki saw this on the agenda, she produced a report on the latest figures. When the item comes up, Nikki is asked for some figures giving predicted sales. She has with her the figures she prepared, but these are not what she is asked for. Confused, she says, 'Sorry, I've brought the latest report—I didn't realise you wanted a prediction.' 'Didn't you read the agenda?' a colleague mutters impatiently. She did, but it hadn't been clear. If only the agenda had been clear, Nikki could have prepared properly, and had what people needed to hand.

Mike's team meeting leaves the members dissatisfied

Mike goes to a team meeting for the first time. Just before the meeting begins, the chairperson calls Mike by telephone to explain she can't make it. 'Can you chair for me?' she asks. 'I'd be really grateful.' Mike agrees, and runs the meeting very efficiently. The meeting takes three-quarters of an hour, whereas usually, meetings run for about two hours. Mike is very pleased with himself. But then, on the way down the corridor, he follows two colleagues from the meeting, and overhears their conversation. 'Well, he's like Atilla the Hun—you can't get a word in edgeways! I shan't be coming any more if meetings are going to be like this from now on!' Mike feels embarrassed. If only he had remembered that meetings don't just have to achieve the business—they also need to satisfy the people present.

DISCUSSION POINTS

1. Think of a meeting you have attended but not chaired. List the good things and bad things that either happened or that the chairperson did. How could things have been handled better?

2. When you next attend a meeting, keep a list of each member's name, and keep score of how many times they speak on each topic. Do some people dominate? Do some people fail to contribute? How could this be changed?

The material on pages 80 to 85 is reproduced with the kind permission of Mr Ritchie Stevenson.

7
Managing Your Team

UNDERSTANDING LEADERSHIP

What is the difference between management and leadership? The dictionary defines **management** as being in charge, controlling, administering, handling. **Leadership**, on the other hand, is defined as being the principal or 'front-runner', being an example, holding the chief role, as well as many of the list of definitions for management. Leadership is more *visible* somehow—the public face of management.

Of course, another consideration is that you cannot be a leader without followers. If you have no people, you can still be a manager (of resources, money, projects etc), but not a leader. A further distinction is that leaders tend to be elected, while managers tend to be appointed.

There are three components to any situation requiring a leader. These are:

- a leader
- a situation
- a group of people.

These three components have led to three theories on leadership. Just because there are three theories, it doesn't mean that only one is right and the other two must be wrong. All three have more than a grain of truth in them.

The leader—trait theory
It used to be thought that leaders were 'born not made'—that they were born with certain **traits** that made them a good leader. People believed leadership was a superiority over others that people were born either with or without. Therefore, a born leader would emerge naturally in any group, because they would have the traits or qualities necessary to be a leader.

The problem with this is that when we look at great leaders in history, the traits they possessed are not all the same. Consider Adolf Hitler and Mahatma Gandhi—both great leaders of their time, but with vastly differing qualities or traits. Physical differences occur too—consider General de Gaulle and Napoleon Bonaparte—one tall, the other short, and both great French leaders.

Improving your trait leadership

Develop your abilities as much as you can. Yes, some abilities you are either born with or not, such as a magnetic personality, but there are many other abilities you can work on:

- ability to see opportunities
- adaptability
- analysis
- communication
- decision-making
- dependability
- enthusiasm
- imagination
- integrity
- open-mindedness
- positive thinking
- reliability
- sincerity
- single-mindedness
- understanding
- willingness

and many, many more.

The situation—situational theory

This theory says that there is no such thing as a born leader, but that there are a whole variety of characteristics that might make a person a good leader, which people have a mixture of. In any situation, the person best suited to that **situation** will emerge as leader.

We can all imagine this—in a crisis, we usually look to someone who knows what to do, or who seems to be in control. In a different situation, exactly the same group of people might look to a completely different person for leadership.

This theory says that leaders rise to *power*—to have authority. There are three main sources of power that a leader can build on: position, personality and expertise.

Position

This is status, position or rank. Some people are seen as powerful because they have status, or are appointed to a certain position or rank. Examples would be Alexander the Great, Queen Victoria or General Custer.

Personality

This is character, or charisma. Some people are seen as powerful because they have a powerful character or personality. Examples would be Lawrence of Arabia, Napoleon Bonaparte, Mahatma Gandhi, John F. Kennedy.

Expertise

This is knowledge, experience or skill. Some people are seen to be powerful because of their knowledge or skill or experience. A good historical example would be Isambard Kingdom Brunel.

Improving your situational leadership

Develop power or authority relevant to situations you commonly find yourself in. If you have low status, develop knowledge and experience to compensate. Try to stay adaptable, so you have something relevant to contribute in all work situations.

- Plan.

- Take advantage of any available training.

- Keep updated about things around you.

- Find out about areas you are weak in.

- Talk to people—try to learn from others.

- Keep in close contact with your boss—keep them up-to-date.

- Learn to work with staff representatives and trade union representatives.

- Get to know other managers and build relationships with them.

- Think ahead, anticipate likely events, then prepare for them.

The group—functional theory

The third theory on leadership, John Adair's theory, says that any group has a number of functions it needs to perform—a number of needs that need to be fulfilled. The leader will be the one who can best satisfy those needs. These needs are in three categories: team, task and individual needs.

- *Team*: The group of people needs to be drawn together and organised so they co-operate with each other.

- *Task*: The task the group is faced with needs to be achieved.

- *Individual*: Individuals need to be recognised and utilised appropriately—they need to use their skills and talents when they can.

A good leader must concentrate on all three functions or needs. Too much attention to the team may mean that individuals become dissatisfied, or the task is not achieved. Too much attention to the task, and the team and individuals may work poorly together, then friction and dissatisfaction may result. Too much attention to individuals, and the team may pull apart, and the task not be achieved.

Improving your functional leadership

Be aware of the three functions, and do not neglect any of them. Acquire knowledge and expertise in dealing with tasks, teams and individuals.

Task
- Set standards, and maintain them.

- Monitor and evaluate performance.

- Set realistic and achievable objectives, both for yourself and for others.

Team
- Let people know that personal gain is not as important as team achievement.

- Communicate regularly.

- Encourage co-operation and compromise in the event of differences among team members.

- Keep everyone informed of progress.

Individual
- Explain what is to be done, why and how.

- Encourage people to be more involved.

- Get to know people.

- Help people develop their skills.

- Delegate wherever possible.

- Recognise people's achievements and contributions.

- Make any criticism constructive.

MOTIVATING OTHERS

You can't be a leader without followers—you need other people. So now we are going to look at how to motivate people.

Motivation is what makes people act in a particular way—what 'makes them tick'. Understanding this is important for a manager, because if you know *why* people do things, it makes it easier to persuade them to do the things you want them to do. It makes it easier to get things done.

One of the main tasks of management is to influence other people to do something—often things they would not normally want to do. Understanding people's **motives**—their reasons for doing or not doing a thing—can help us do this.

Basically, people have **needs**. A need is a lack of something —something we want. This produces a **drive**, or a motive in us to satisfy that need. This motivates us. Satisfying this need, or getting the thing we want or lack, is our **goal**.

Needs

Maslow's theory of motivation is called the 'hierarchy of needs'. Maslow thought that people have five main needs in the following order of importance:

- *Physiological needs*   —the need to eat
  - —the need to drink
  - —the need to work
  - —the need to sleep
  - —the need to reproduce

- *Safety needs*   —the need for shelter
  - —the need to feel secure

- *'Belonging' needs*   —the need to feel part of a group
  - —the need for acceptance

- *Self-esteem needs*   —the need to feel good about themselves
  - —the need to be recognised for achievement

- *Self-realisation needs*   —the need for personal fulfilment
  - —the need to grow and develop

Maslow believed that people would not move on down this list to be motivated by the next set of needs until the previous set(s) had been satisfied.

Another theory—by Alderfer—categorised these needs into only three groups:

- existence needs

- relatedness needs

- growth needs.

This simplifies the issue—we have needs to maintain us physically, needs to relate to others, and needs to develop and grow as individuals.

Remember, everyone is different—some people come to work to earn money (existence needs) and have no desire either to 'get on' with others (relatedness needs), or earn promotion (growth needs). Others work to meet people and have a personal challenge and sense of achievement (relatedness needs). Others work to gain experience to move their career forward (growth needs). Obviously, many people work for a combination of reasons.

Motivating people by filling existence needs

- Pay people appropriately for the work they do.

- Make sure the workplace is safe, and a good environment to work in.

- Give people enough work to do.

- Give people incentives—prizes or bonuses. Beware—this can be dangerous, as some people will not respond, and some will be demotivated because they think they have no chance of 'winning'.

- Recognise people's need for privacy—give them their 'own space'.

- Try to arrange work so people see the end result.

- Set goals so people know what they are doing.

- Treat people as individuals.

Motivating people by filling relatedness needs

- Show respect for people—listen to them and express an interest in them.

- Give people responsibility—delegate.

- Give recognition—thank people, and acknowledge achievement and effort.

- Communicate openly with people.

- Involve people in decision-making.

- Encourage ideas and suggestions.

- Praise people for effort as well as achievement—a thing doesn't have to be perfect to be praised.

- Get to know people and make sure they know others.

- Keep in contact—exchange information regularly.

Motivating people by filling growth needs

● Offer support and help to do new tasks.

● Give people a challenge where possible.

● Make work interesting.

● Encourage people to think for themselves.

● Keep people informed about new information and developments appropriate to them.

● Ask people what motivates them, and give them the chance to do it whenever possible.

● Give people new work, when possible, to 'stretch' them.

● Offer training when possible. This does not have to be a course—you can do things like advise them on reading, or set up sessions where people work with others to learn more about others' work.

QUESTIONS AND ANSWERS

How can you tell if people are motivated or not?
If people are not motivated (demotivated), you may see some of the following:

● increased sickness
● increased absenteeism
● lateness
● poor quality work
● lack of communication
● attitude
● emotional levels rise—frustration, short-temperedness etc.

So why do people become demotivated?
● lack of recognition
● boredom/lack of interest or stimulation
● lack of involvement
● not being listened to

- lack of encouragement
- lack of training
- poor or no delegation
- criticism
- too much or too little work.

If I had to pick one thing that motivates people, which is the most important?

Recognition. Most other factors involve recognition in some way. Demotivated people may be late, for example, or absent, or get angry and short-tempered in order to be noticed. This is nothing more than a disguised search for recognition, which the individuals may not even be aware of. So, recognition produces motivation, while lack of recognition demotivates people.

WORKING AS A TEAM

Why work as a team?

Creativity
- Teams are usually more creative than individuals.

- Teams tend to produce more ideas.

Satisfaction
- Teamworking can provide good opportunities for personal development and learning.

- Individuals find increased motivation from working in a team.

- Responsibility is shared, so individuals feel more committed to the work.

- Energy and excitement tends to be greater.

- A sense of belonging and pride can be generated.

- A team contains a larger range of experience and abilities than any one individual.

Skills
- Skills and abilities can be utilised fully.

- Some tasks simply cannot be done by an individual.

Speed/productivity
- Things can be done faster—'many hands make light work'.

- Productivity is usually higher, as teamwork focuses effort and skills.

- A wider range of work can be undertaken.

Evaluation
- Teams evaluate ideas from more viewpoints than an individual could, so ideas tend to be better evaluated.

- Analysis and judgement can be more objective in a team, although teams can take more risks, as individuals feel less personally responsible.

Obviously, there are many tasks which it would not be appropriate to carry out as a team. Simple or routine tasks are best dealt with by individuals, and also decisions which can be logically calculated or deduced.

Selecting a team size

The size of team you should use varies—there are advantages and disadvantages of having large or small teams. Consider the following points when deciding how many to include in your team:

- *Vulnerability*: The smaller the team, the more vulnerable it is— replacing just one team member can upset the whole team, and one member being absent can be critical. In a large team, substitutions and absences can be handled more easily.

- *Relationships*: The smaller the team, the closer the relationships between team members.

- *Individuality*: The larger the team, the less individuality members have. A large team can take on 'mob mentality', where people stop thinking of themselves, and simply go along with the team, regardless of whether they would normally agree or not. The larger the group, the greater the pressure for conformity.

- *Control*: The larger the team, the harder it is to control—the more organisation and direction it needs. With large teams, a structure may need to be developed, with sub-groups.

SETTING OBJECTIVES

The best way to make sure people stay focused on a task is to set objectives, for individuals as well as for teams. Objectives are performance goals or targets. They are specific results or situations that a person or group is expected to achieve within a given time-frame.

Setting objectives is important for several reasons:

- They show individuals and teams what direction to work towards.

- They give a means of measuring achievement.

- They motivate—people are motivated by achievement and recognition.

- They prevent wasted effort.

How to set objectives

1. Agree objectives jointly. Remember, people are more committed to a thing, and more likely to take responsibility, if they have been involved in it.

2. Agree the measures of achievement. If an objective cannot be measured, you will not be able to assess whether it has been achieved or not.

3. Be specific if possible. The more specific you are, the easier it will be to see whether the objective has been achieved satisfactorily.

4. Agree a realistic time scale. If you don't set a time limit, it may never get done.

5. Make the objectives achievable but challenging. Setting unrealistic objectives is demotivating.

6. Let the person who is to achieve the objective decide how to do it.

7. Use objectives for personal development—to stretch and teach people.

8. Review progress regularly.

CHECKLIST

- Try and improve your leadership skills.

- Be aware of tasks, teams and individuals, and give them all an appropriate amount of attention.

- Be aware of people's needs and motives—including your own.

- Motivate people appropriately—remember not everyone is motivated by the same things.

- Tackle demotivation—if you leave it, it may spread to others.

- Give recognition wherever possible.

- Work as a team.

- Set objectives—for yourself, for others and for teams.

- Monitor performance by whether objectives are being met, and give recognition where possible.

CASE STUDIES

Bev's 'team' excludes the cook

After her disastrous meeting, Bev decides to have short team meetings once a week to try to make the shift feel more like a team. She decides to have the meetings on Mondays, for the first fifteen minutes of the shift, before work starts. This is a time when the cook, Sarah, is exceptionally busy, having just done breakfasts and being required to start lunch preparation, so she is unable to attend. After a while, Sarah leaves. Bev is sorry, but feels even worse when she hears from some of the other staff that Sarah felt left out of things, and that she never had any support and assistance. If only Bev had realised the importance of including everybody, Sarah wouldn't have felt so miserable and left her job.

Nikki decides to try to motivate her staff

Nikki buys some books for the office, and takes photocopies of any relevant articles in professional magazines to pass round the office to keep people up-to-date. She gives them more demanding work to do whenever she can, giving them a challenge and more responsibility. She sets up a 'shadowing' programme, where they each spend one day a week with another member of staff, learning about their job.

Jacquie doesn't respond, and seems, if anything, less motivated than before Nikki started her efforts. When Nikki asks Jacquie whether anything is wrong, Jacquie says, 'I don't feel involved in all these decisions you're making about my job, Nikki. I don't want to take on more—I took this job because I liked it, and I liked working with the people in the office. Now nobody has time to talk to anybody any more.' If only Nikki had remembered that there is little point in working on higher needs unless the lower needs have been satisfied. Jacquie is motivated by social needs, and just wants to do her job well, and work with people she likes. She isn't motivated by advancement or development.

Mike loses his leadership

Mike sets individual objectives monthly, and he allocates all the work as it comes in. Any large tasks he tends to split into small sections of work, and give these to individuals. He has always tried to set work appropriate to each individual's skills and experience. One day, he chances on some work on Rachel's desk whilst she is out of the office. It is work he knows he allocated to Tom. On investigation, it turns out that the others are re-allocating work behind his back, so each person does the jobs they *like* best. Mike has lost control—he has lost his leadership. If only he had looked more to the team and the individuals, rather than the most efficient way to achieve the task all the time, this might not have happened.

DISCUSSION POINTS

1. Go through the list of traits that a leader can develop. Write objectives to help you develop those you need to improve on. For example: *Open-mindedness*—develop my open-mindedness by encouraging others to make suggestions to me and considering each fully. Aim to double the amount of suggestions I receive each week within six months.

2. Do you ever feel demotivated? Why? What can you do to prevent this in others?

3. Examine any teams you are a part of. Do they work well, or not? Why?

8
Managing Staff

Figure 13 shows the sequence of defining and filling a job. Time could be saved by omitting one or more steps, but only by doing each step will you be sure of appointing the best person for the job. You also need to ensure you have been fair and complied with relevant employment legislation and not been discriminatory in any way.

DEFINING WHO AND WHAT YOU WANT

Considering options
When a vacancy arises, you don't necessarily just have to recruit a replacement: other options might be better. Consider the following:

Part-time/full-time
Could several part-time staff do the job of one full-time staff? This can give more flexibility.

Temporary/permanent/fixed term contract
Is a permanent replacement necessary? If the future is uncertain, temporary staff or a fixed term contract (a contract until a certain date) might be beneficial.

Secondment
Could someone in another department or section gain experience from doing the job for a while (a **secondment**)?

Redistribution of duties
Could the work be done by redistributing it amongst existing staff? If it could, this could save money.

Describing jobs and people
After reviewing the options, the next stage is to produce a **job description** and **person specification**. These are written descriptions of the job and the person you want to do it, that you use to help

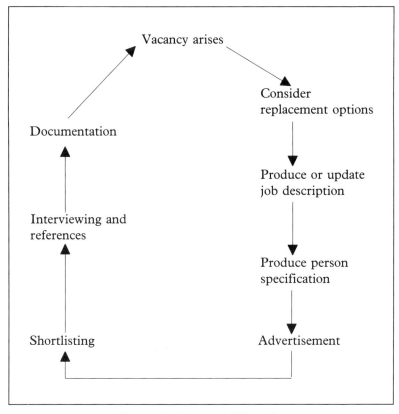

Fig. 13. Defining and filling jobs.

you choose the right person for the job. The person specification is especially important in helping you avoid discrimination.

Job descriptions

If you are simply replacing someone, you may already have a job description. If so, it must be checked so it is up-to-date and accurately reflects what you actually want the new person to do.

If you don't already have a job description, for example if it is a new job, it is good practice to produce one. Many organisations have a standard format for this, but the main points to be included are set out below.

Remember, when the successful person accepts the job, you should get them to sign a copy of the job description, to show they accept these duties as the job, and they agree to carry out all the duties listed.

The job
- Job title
- Department and section

Purpose
- The purpose of the job
- Objectives of the job (quantified where possible)
- Duties involved and methods of carrying them out

Responsibilities
- Any responsibility for developing or recommending changes
- Responsibilities for equipment, people, money etc

Relationships
- Who the job liaises with
- To whom the job is accountable
- Other relationships that influence achievement of objectives

Physical conditions
- Where the job is
- Hours of work
- Accident or health risks

Pay and conditions
- Salary range
- Bonus or incentive schemes if any
- Pensions
- Sickness entitlement
- Holiday entitlement
- Car or other allowances

Any other duties
- It is good practice to include an 'any other duties' clause, stating that the post-holder is required to carry out any other duties within reason. This enables you to give them duties that are not in their job description when necessary—it gives you flexibility.

Describing people

The person specification is the job description translated into human terms. Without this, you cannot define the type of person you are looking for.

You simply list the essential requirements, or **criteria**. Human nature means that we often tend to come up with a specification for superman or superwoman, and no one could ever match this, so try to keep criteria realistic. Criteria should only be set if the job could not be performed to the required standard without them.

The person specification need not be a formal document, but ensure the following do not get overlooked:

Physical factors
- What are the requirements in terms of physical ability and health?
- Consider height, build, hearing, eyesight, general health.
- Requirements in terms of appearance.
- Consider looks, grooming, dress, voice.
- Beware of prejudice.

Skills and knowledge
- What knowledge and skills are needed to do the job?
- What qualifications are needed?
- What experience or past training is needed?
- How much experience in other jobs is required?

Emotional factors
- How important is it that the person be able to get on with others?
- What ability for leadership is needed?
- Is stability (steadiness and dependability) important?
- Is self-reliance—independent thought and working—necessary?

Personal circumstances
- Is mobility needed?
- Is nearness of home to the job relevant?
- Do they need to be able to work irregular hours?
- What personal circumstances would prevent someone from doing the job?
- Again, be especially aware of prejudice and discrimination in this area.

Make a list of all the factors on a sheet of paper. Mark each item as **essential** or **desirable**. Essential shows a person could not do the job without it. Desirable simply means you would prefer the person to fit your list in this respect, but they could still do the job if they didn't.

Now you have a good profile of who you want—what sort of person. By comparing people with your list, you can be sure you will choose the right person, *objectively*, without prejudice or discrimination.

ADVERTISING

There are many ways of advertising vacancies. The most usual are:

- adverts in a newspaper or magazine

- cards in Jobcentres

- cards in shop windows

- noticeboards

- recruitment or advertising agencies (note that these normally charge you a fee for finding you the right person)

- staff newsletters.

Do not forget to advertise internally. Someone working in another part of your organisation might want to apply, or a member of staff may know someone looking for a similar job. Internal advertising is usually free.

Remember that advertising in newspapers and magazines can be expensive. Unless you are in a rush, you could always try cheaper methods first (such as noticeboards, shop windows or Jobcentres), to see whether you get a good response, before moving on to expensive advertising in papers and magazines.

Content of advertisements

Whatever method you decide on, be as specific and detailed as possible in your advertisement. This will give you as suitable a group of applicants as possible. It is a waste of time and money dealing with unsuitable applicants. Be sure to include:

- where the job is

- the salary or pay

- the hours

- any essential criteria such as a requirement for shorthand or particular qualifications

- a date by which to apply

- how you would like them to apply
  —by letter
  —by sending a curriculum vitae (CV)
  —by telephone
  —in person
  —on an application form.

SHORTLISTING APPLICANTS

Step one—compare with the person specification

Once you have all the applications, go through each one against the person specification. Use a copy of your list of factors, and eliminate any applications that do not fit all the essential criteria. These can be written a polite letter saying their application has been unsuccessful.

Step two—selecting the final shortlist

All applications that fit all the essential criteria should now be compared to the desirable criteria. Draw a column on your sheet with your criteria on it for each name, and tick the criteria they fit. You should be able to see at a glance who fits best the criteria list, by the number of ticks.

This method minimises the risk of unfair discrimination. You should keep a note of your decisions at this stage, and keep this with all the applications for at least six months. This is in case anyone alleges you discriminated unfairly, or takes you to an industrial tribunal.

A polite letter can now go to those you have eliminated from your shortlist.

Step three—arranging the interview

Invitations
- Write a letter or make a telephone call to those successfully shortlisted, inviting them to an interview.

- Make sure you have enough people to choose from—if you plan to interview three people, and one does not attend, you only have a choice of two. Keep your options open.

- Some organisations send shortlisted applicants some information about the job and the organisation. This will help the applicants decide whether they still want to apply for the job or not.

- Give people enough notice about the interview, and give them directions.

References
It is usual to ask for references before interview (although some organisations do this afterwards). Schools do not usually give written references for school-leavers, except for the 'records of achievement'.

Detailed arrangements
Make sure the room is vacant and you will not be disturbed. Make sure reception staff know who is expected and when. Arrange for somewhere for people to wait before their interview.

AVOIDING DISCRIMINATION

You must not discriminate against people in particular groups unless the law specifically permits this. Basically, these groups are:

- women (including pregnant women)

- men

- married people

- people of a particular 'race' (colour, ethnic or national origin)

- people with disabilities

- people with 'spent' (out-of-date) criminal convictions

- people who belong to or will not belong to a trade union.

Direct discrimination includes:

- specifying different criteria for different groups which are not justified

- deliberately setting out to exclude persons who belong to a particular group.

Indirect discrimination includes things such as:

- setting criteria which exclude large numbers of a particular group,

because less people in that group would be able to meet the
criteria

- using tests which are not necessary for success at the job—this
may discriminate against people whose first language is not
English

- requiring some groups to undertake tests which other groups do
not have to perform

- asking questions of one group which you do not ask of another
group.

If someone feels that have been unfairly discriminated against, they
can take you to an industrial tribunal.

INTERVIEWING

Interviews have two **aims**:

- To confirm and expand on the information you already have
about the applicant.

- To give the applicant more information about the job.

Interviews may sound simple, but they are **difficult** for two reasons:

- The interviewer only has a limited amount of time to find out all
they need.

- Interviews are stressful. This may cause both interviewer and
interviewee to behave unnaturally.

To overcome this, the interviewer needs to remember several **key
points**:

- Control the interview by questioning.

- Establish rapport to reduce the stress, so the interviewee can be
as natural as possible.

- Listen and observe. Be sensitive to all information.

- Prepare thoroughly, so interview time is used to best advantage.

- Structure the content of the interview so they get the information they want.

QUESTIONS AND ANSWERS

I worry about what sorts of questions to ask at interviews. What sort are best?
Questions should be aimed at assessing people's suitability against the essential or desirable criteria you have set. They should be mainly about work experience, qualifications, skills, abilities and aptitudes. They should relate to the requirements of the job. If personal circumstances may affect performance in the job (e.g. if working unsocial hours is required), this should be discussed objectively without detailed questions about family circumstances. Questions which may imply discrimination must be avoided.

Can I really ask questions about all my criteria? Some of them are difficult to ask about without being personal, or possibly discriminating?
Genuine criteria which it may prove the most difficult to probe (because valid questions may be misinterpreted) are those relating to availability during all likely working hours, commitment to a regular permanent job, or career aspirations. If you have to probe these matters, put questions in such a way that they apply equally to all interviewees. Then, actually ask them of all interviewees, not just some. Examples would be:

1. Have you any commitments that might mean you need time off other than for holidays?

2. How long do you intend remaining in this job?

How can I be sure I have not discriminated unfairly?
Remember, it is not sufficient for an interviewer to *think* they have not discriminated unfairly, or to *believe* they have used fair criteria. It must be possible to *show*, if challenged, that rational criteria were applied, and that applicants have no valid reason for feeling discrimination has happened. Thus, you need to know the job requirements, to judge against them and only them, and to keep records for at least six months after an appointment is made. Records

should include references, and notes made at interview. Therefore, interviewers should note briefly in writing why the successful applicant was chosen, and if possible, why the others were not.

INDUCTING NEW EMPLOYEES

When new staff start work, they need to know many things before they are truly settled in and their work is productive. To ensure that they are able to contribute to the organisation as quickly as possible, set time aside to **induct** them—to make them part of the organisation.

Research shows that new people are most likely to leave within their first few weeks, so concentrate on making them feel part of the team at the earliest opportunity. Your organisation may have an **induction course** for new employees. If so, do not assume it covers everything—still check if there is anything you need to cover yourself.

As a rough guide, try to cover all of the following with new employees. This should give them a good induction to work.

Documentation and procedures
● Completion of time sheets or clocking arrangements.

● Payday and method of payment.

● Bonus, productivity or incentive schemes.

● What to do in the event of sickness or absence.

● How to book holidays.

Introductions
● Introductions to colleagues.

● Introduction to their job—main duties.

● Introduction to contacts outside immediate workplace, if any.

● Introduction to supervisor and/or manager.

Working arrangements
● Workplace.

● Hours of work.

- Tea and coffee breaks.

- Canteen, cloakroom, staff room and toilet facilities etc.

- Issue of any equipment, tools etc.

- Relation of their job to others' work.

Emergency and safety
- Emergency procedures.

- Fire precautions and drills.

- First aid location.

- Safety policy, procedures and practices.

General information
- Description of department, section, organisation.

- Structure of department or section and names of key personnel.

- Trade union membership—where to join.

- Holidays—entitlement, timing etc.

- Pension/superannuation—rate of deductions etc.

- Grievance procedures—how to make a grievance.

- Disciplinary procedures, and workplace rules etc.

- Available training schemes.

- Personnel policies.

The best thing of all is to make **time** for the new person. Try to set aside some time every day for at least the first week or so, to talk to them and see how they are doing.

TRAINING PEOPLE

Why train people?
● To enable the job to be done properly.

● To maintain quality.

● To maintain quantity.

● To meet legal requirements.

● To give management flexibility.

● To develop a member of staff.

● To give someone a boost—increase morale and motivation.

● To prepare someone for a forthcoming change in job/work.

People don't need to go away on a training course—there are many ways of training people, including working alongside an experienced employee (on the job training), following manuals and instruction books, project work, secondments and teamworking.

Fig. 14 shows the training cycle, the various stages of which are explained in the following paragraphs.

Training needs analysis
A **training need** is a shortfall in performance that training could correct. Talk to people and see what they feel they lack in terms of skills, knowledge and understanding. Then look at their performance and experience, and see what you feel they lack in terms of skills, knowledge and experience. Fig. 15 shows the equation.

Many organisations use appraisals as an opportunity to discuss training needs. However, training needs don't always occur just before appraisals, so be watchful for them at any time.

Set objectives for the training need, so you and the person to be trained both know what you will get out of it. For example:

Training need: Needs to be able to use new word processor.

Objective: To be able to use new word processor unsupervised, but with occasional reference to the manual, after attending two-day training course.

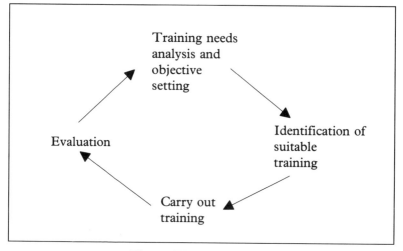

Fig. 14. The training cycle.

Identification of suitable training
Find out how to train the person to fill the training need.

- Can you teach them yourself?

- Can they read what they need to know from manuals or books?

- Is there a training course?

- Could they work with someone experienced and learn from them?

Carry out the training
Give the person a date and time when they will be trained and stick to it. Make sure the person carrying out the training knows what objective(s) you have set for the trainee.

Evaluation
After training has taken place, evaluate. This means check whether the training has worked or not—don't assume that just because someone has been trained the objective has now been met and everything will be all right. Go back to the objective(s) you set and ask whether they have been met. If not, you may have to take a look at further training or extra support.

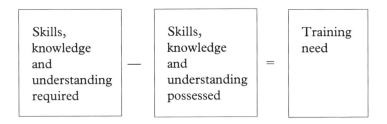

Fig. 15. Training needs analysis equation.

CHECKLIST

● Define exactly who and what you want before starting to look for it.

● Don't automatically replace someone with a similar person. Consider all your options for getting that work done.

● Make advertisements specific, so you attract a set of applicants that are very close to what you are looking for. This will save you time.

● Use the criteria to shortlist, and keep records.

● Be objective, and try to avoid discriminating.

● Induct new employees properly.

● When training needs are detected, act to fill them with appropriate training.

CASE STUDIES

Bev replaces Sarah the cook with June

Bev doesn't bother drawing up a person specification, thinking she has a good idea of what she is looking for. At the interviews, however, June stands out as a good applicant to Bev, perhaps because she is so similar to Sarah in a lot of ways. After a few weeks, it becomes apparent that June is a disaster. She is always taking time off, unlike Sarah, who was responsible about such things. If only Bev had been objective and recruited someone who was suitable, rather than someone she liked.

Nikki's trainee annoys a senior manager

Nikki has a college trainee, Frances, to work in the office for three months. Nikki doesn't send her on the company induction course as she will only be with them a short time, but Nikki inducts Frances about the fire exits etc. A few weeks after Frances' work placement is over, a senior manager comes in waving a report. 'Just look at this!' he exclaims. 'Frances obviously doesn't have a clue what this company does, and has written a report for college saying we're badly organised. If she'd known why we're structured like this, she wouldn't have written something like this. She draws the conclusion we're structured wrongly, and some work is duplicated, wasting us money. It looks very bad for the company! The Managing Director is furious!' If only Frances had been inducted properly, it could all have been avoided.

Mike's training isn't effective

A new computer system is installed, so Mike arranges some training. After the training, people still can't quite use the system properly, but Rachel seems to have got the hang of it, so people tend to go to her for advice. Rachel helps them use the system, but then one day, some data has to be transferred to another section, and the system just won't do it. Eventually, the data has to be printed out and given to the other section to re-enter. This will obviously take the other section quite some time. If only Mike had evaluated the training. This is often the most important thing—to check that the training has actually worked.

DISCUSSION POINTS

1. Choose a member of staff at work. If they left tomorrow, how many different ways could you arrange for their workload to be carried out?

2. With the same member of staff in mind, assume you are replacing them. Draw up a new job description, or go through their current one and see whether this is what you really want. Draw up a person specification.

3. Going back to point 2, compare the job description and person specification with the member of staff you currently have. How do they differ? Draw up a training needs analysis for the person to address any differences between their current skills, knowledge and experience and those you want.

9
Managing People Problems

APPRAISING STAFF

Appraisals are reviews of an employee's performance. They are generally in the form of a one-to-one interview with their manager or supervisor at regular intervals, from which a written record is made. Your organisation may have its own appraisal or performance review system, but you can also do your own, even if no formal system exists.

Why do appraisals?
- To objectively examine an individual's performance over a given period of time.

- To get feedback from an individual on how they think they are doing, and their hopes for the future.

- To agree future performance targets.

What are the advantages of appraisals?

For the employee
- They learn how they are getting on (their performance).
- It ensures their efforts are acknowledged and appreciated.
- It identifies improvements that need to be made in performance.
- It maps out future career prospects.

For the manager
- Better understanding of employees.
- Better co-operation from staff.
- It reviews performance of staff.
- They gain an insight into the employee's ideas about the job.
- It helps identify future potential.

For the organisation
- It makes staff more committed.
- Personal relationships improve.
- Effectiveness and efficiency improve.
- It helps to plan future allocation of work.

How to carry out an appraisal interview

1. Review the person's file and history in advance. Look at their job description.

2. Make arrangements for the interview in advance.

- Book a room where you will not be disturbed.
- Give the person notice of the appraisal.
- Reassure them—many people find appraisals nerve-wracking.

3. Carry out the interview as informally as possible. Let them participate. Discuss:

- *Past*   —how they think they've done
              —how they have done

- *Present*   —how they think they're doing
              —how they are doing

- *Future*   —what they would like to do or think they might do
              —what you think they should do or could do.

4. Agree a plan of action. Set objectives.

5. Write a record of the interview (and ideally, get the person to sign it).

6. Monitor and help them throughout the next period, so they can achieve the action plan and objectives set for them.

Why do appraisals go wrong?
- Failure to prepare enough.

- Failure to prepare at all.

- Failure to face up to or tackle problem areas.

- Failure to tackle problems constructively (getting personal).

- Failure to agree on a realistic course of action.

- Failure to take the appraisal seriously.

HANDLING GRIEVANCES

A **grievance** is a formal or official complaint made by an employee. Even if not made in writing, take these seriously. Some organisations have a grievance procedure for you to follow. In any event, a good rule would be to always follow these steps.

1. *Listen*: listen fully to the complaint and acknowledge it.

2. *Investigate*: see whether the complaint is founded or not. Be objective.

3. *Take action*: address the source of the complaint if possible. If the complaint turns out to be unfounded, take action to prove this to the employee.

4. *Feedback*: always tell the person who made the complaint or grievance what you are going to do about it and why. Do this even if you are going to do nothing. Preferably, feedback to them in writing—give them a written copy of what you tell them.

QUESTIONS AND ANSWERS

What happens if someone complains during an appraisal?
Grievances should not be dealt with at appraisals. Appraisals are for discussing the employee who is having the appraisal, not others or their manager. Similarly, disciplinary matters should not be discussed at appraisal, but should be handled separately. By keeping discipline and grievance separate from appraisal, appraisals will be more con-structive. If the complaint is about something specific that you can quickly and easily deal with, fine. But if it is 'messy', or a complaint about someone rather than something, keep it separate.

If an employee keeps complaining after I have answered their complaint, do I have to keep taking it seriously?
If there are a lot of minor complaints, it depends on what they are

about. Don't confuse a grumble with an official complaint. An employee wishing to make an official complaint, or grievance, should be asked to put it in writing so a record can be kept, and if they take it seriously themselves, they will. Minor grumbles are part of life, and should be dealt with on a less formal basis. How do you tell whether the complaint is serious or not? Well, if they are prepared to put it in writing, they usually view it as serious.

Do I have to have a proper interview for an appraisal? I don't really have the time.

No, of course not. There is nothing wrong with just having a quick chat now and again, but most people appreciate you taking the time to have a short interview with them, in private, to discuss their performance and prospects. Otherwise, a regular short chat is sufficient, provided you allow for privacy if someone needs it to discuss something.

DEALING WITH PERFORMANCE PROBLEMS

Sometimes a performance problem can be dealt with at appraisal. More often, it needs dealing with separately—it would be ridiculous to 'save up' problems for the appraisal once every year or six months! If people aren't performing satisfactorily, talk to them.

Identifying the gap

Specify exactly what the gap is between their performance and the required performance. Ideally, get them to agree that there is a gap—then they are far more likely to do something about it. Ways of proving that a gap exists include:

● customer complaints
● others doing similar work for comparison
● record cards
● rejected work
● sickness and absence records
● testimony of people who come into contact with them
● time sheets
● training needs analysis
● unfinished work.

Establishing reasons for the gap

There are many reasons for poor performance. Some of them are listed below:

- domestic circumstances
- emotional problems
- family problems
- job has changed
- lack of intellectual ability
- lack of motivation
- lack of physical ability
- lack of training
- lack of understanding
- personality clash with boss
- personality clash with others
- poor discipline
- poor health
- poor management
- poor pay
- too little confidence
- too much confidence
- unreliable equipment.

Try to establish which reason(s) apply, and whether they are in your control, or not. They may be outside the individual's control, so the gap cannot be closed at present; for example, in the case of poor health.

Closing the gap
Set objectives for closing the gap—in stages if necessary. Review these regularly, reviewing progress.

What to do about unresolved problems
If a problem is not resolved after a reasonable period of time, you should consider taking disciplinary action.

DISPENSING DISCIPLINE

Disciplinary procedures
Most organisations have a disciplinary procedure, which you need to follow whenever you have a disciplinary problem. Most procedures follow stages. A common sequence is this:

1. *Informal warning/discussion*: an informal, 'off-the-record' talk about the problem.

2. *Verbal warning*: this is usually the first stage of **formal** procedures. A verbal warning is given, and a note saying that this has been done is placed on the employee's record or file.

3. *Written warning*: the employee is given a warning in writing, detailing the problem. A copy is placed on the employee's record or file.

4. *Final warning*: this is the same as a written warning, but the employee is warned that any further occurrence of the problem will lead to dismissal.

5. *Dismissal*: this is usually a last resort. The employee is dismissed. This usually follows a final warning, but sometimes for a very serious breach of discipline, an employee could be suspended or dismissed immediately, without going through the other stages. This is referred to as **instant dismissal**.

Preventing disciplinary problems

● Be approachable—that way you find out about problems before they occur or become serious.

● Be consistent and fair.

● Ensure people know all the rules and standards:
—at induction
—at regular intervals.

● Establish good relationships—get to know people.

● Feedback regularly—let people know how they are doing.

● Foster teamwork.

● Remember the importance of recognition—praise people when they do well.

● Set a good example.

● Set targets and make sure people are aware of them.

● Train people adequately to do the job.

Dealing with disciplinary problems

Procedures
- Know your organisation's procedures.

- Know your part in those procedures.

- Know the limits of your authority—when do you need to call for more senior management to get involved?

Timing
- Deal with things as soon as possible—'nip things in the bud' before they get worse.

- Deal with things in private—never discipline in front of others if you can possibly avoid it.

- Don't put things off because they are unpleasant.

- Don't rush things—you have to give the person the opportunity to speak and explain.

- Put a time limit on their improvement—set a date.

Practicalities
- Stay calm and objective. If you find yourself becoming angry, call a break and set a time to speak to them again, when you have calmed down.

- Be prepared. Have all the information and facts at hand. They may deny there is a problem, and so be prepared to prove it to them.

- Don't become subjective—you are dealing with a practical problem, not personalities. Stay focused on what the problem is.

- Get them to talk to you.

- Keep written records of what was said and done. Tell the person what will go on their record or personal file, so they know where they stand.

Monitoring and review

- Don't 'breathe down people's necks' after a disciplinary action. It is very demotivating. You do need to keep an eye on them, but don't make them think they are being watched.

- Praise them when they improve.

- If they do not improve within the agreed time scale, be ready to progress to the next stage of the disciplinary process.

COUNSELLING PEOPLE

Counselling is:

- analysing a problem
- assisting with stimulating someone's thoughts
- giving someone your undivided attention
- identifying with someone
- listening
- providing support.

Counselling is *not* about:

- giving advice
- giving opinions
- imposing your beliefs or emotions
- judging
- making suggestions.

Why counsel people?

Most people are capable of sorting out their own problems and crises. Some aren't. For these people, just talking things over with someone can be a great help.

How to counsel someone

If someone has a problem and wants to talk it over with you, always remember the following:

- Accept and tolerate their confusion.

- Allow the person to make their own decision.

- Check you understand, and confirm you are both on the same wavelength.

- Empathise with them—try to see things through their eyes.

- Establish the facts and what options they have.

- Give the person encouragement and confidence to keep talking.

- Give the person the space they need to explore the problem for themselves. This means not talking too much.

- Leave a way open for the person to talk to you again if they wish.

- Make the person feel you are there for them.

- Open up other avenues of thought they may not have considered.

- Respond in a genuine, caring manner.

- Say you are pleased they felt able to talk to you.

- Show interest.

- Show you understand their difficulty.

- Stress confidentiality.

- Try and clarify confused thoughts.

What to avoid
Try not to do any of the following:

- Appear shocked by anything that is said.

- Come up with premature suggestions.

- Discuss the person with others (unless they agree you may).

- Give advice or express your own views.

- Let your own values, perceptions and attitudes get in the way.

- Make the person feel inferior or inadequate.

- Make personal judgements.

- Stop the free flow of conversation.

CHECKLIST

- Appraise people regularly—informally as well as formally.

- Always take employee complaints and/or grievances seriously.

- Deal with performance problems as soon as they arise.

- Always be seen to be fair.

- Remember, discipline is not about judgement or punishment. It is about getting performance right—closing the gap.

- Make time for people—counselling doesn't have to be formal. Listen to people and show an interest—sometimes it can help a great deal.

CASE STUDIES

Bev fails to use correct disciplinary procedures

Bev repeatedly has to warn Karen about her lack of acceptable performance. Just about everything she does seems to be below standard. After a while, Matron and Bev discuss the situation, and Bev wants to dismiss Karen. Unfortunately, Bev's warnings have all been informal, and 'off-the-record'. As there is no record of Karen having been warned, all they can do is give her a verbal warning, and wait until next time to issue a written warning. If only Bev had taken action at the beginning, Karen would either have improved, or Matron would have been able to dismiss her.

Nikki starts doing staff appraisals

Appraisals are a new experience for Nikki's section. At the appraisals, it is obvious that people are focused on how they have done—the past. They are reluctant to discuss the future and their prospects. Nikki gets frustrated by people's negative expectations. If only she had remembered that many people find appraisals frightening, and expect to be told how badly they have done, and to have their mistakes pointed out to them. Speaking to people, and reassuring them about what the appraisals were trying to achieve, would have helped here.

Mike is seen as unfair

Mike establishes a gap in Tom's performance. He sets objectives, and waits for an improvement. After a period of time, there is no noticeable change in Tom's work. Mike also hears that other staff are 'behind Tom', and think that Mike has been very unfair. Tom has obviously been talking about the situation to the others. If only Mike had got Tom to accept the gap. If people don't accept that there is a gap, they will feel victimised and frustrated.

DISCUSSION POINTS

1. Choose a member of staff at work, and imagine you have to appraise them next week. Objectively assess their performance in terms of past, present and future.

2. Choose a member of staff with a real or imaginary performance problem. Identify the gap, and think of how you could establish this gap so they accept it exists. How would you establish the reasons for the gap—what would you ask them? Set some objectives to close the gap.

3. Imagine that the performance problem has not improved. How does your organisation's disciplinary process tell you to proceed?

10
Managing Customers

UNDERSTANDING CUSTOMERS AND SERVICE

Your customers are your organisation's reason for existing. Whether you have individual customers purchasing goods and services from you, or have other organisations who obtain goods and services from you, or just deal with staff from other parts of your organisation (called **internal customers**)—customer service is important.

Whenever you deal with people outside your work, whether face-to-face, by telephone or in writing, you should remember one thing—the **image** of your work. You *are* your organisation as far as the other person is concerned. How you react to them will influence their view of your organisation as a whole—it will affect your organisation's image.

Customer service is often referred to as **customer care**.

What makes good customer care?

● Courteous staff.

● Friendly staff.

● Helpful (but not pushy) staff.

● Informative staff, who keep customers informed without needing to be chased.

● Knowledgeable staff.

● Professional staff.

● Responsible staff.

● Staff who behave as if they care about the customer.

- Staff who do not lose their ability to perform under pressure.

- Staff who do not reduce the service they offer under pressure.

- Staff who do what they say they will.

- Staff who listen.

- Staff who promote a good image of their product, service, work or organisation.

- Staff who respond promptly.

Spot the obvious? The word **staff** appears every time. Yes, people come to you for a product or service, but what makes them remember your organisation is the staff. The best product or service can be ruined by the worst staff, and vice versa.

The importance of internal customers

We are often so keen to deal well with those outside the organisation that we neglect our internal customers. Late information, non-returned telephone calls, unanswered internal memos all indicate poor customer care to internal customers. And the most ironic thing is that they may need your information or answer in order to service a 'real', external customer of their own—you end up providing bad service to those you wanted to serve best.

DEALING WITH PEOPLE BY TELEPHONE

- Answer the telephone as quickly as possible.

- Give telephone calls your full attention—don't read or carry on with other work whilst speaking.

- Identify yourself by name, section, job title or the form your organisation usually uses.

- If the right person isn't available, offer to take a message—don't wait to be asked.

- If you have to put someone on hold:
  —explain why
  —reassure them now and again that you haven't forgotten them

—thank them for waiting once you take their call back

—never put someone on hold without asking their permission first.

- Keep information handy—have information to hand before making a call.

- Listen not only to what they say, but *how* they say it—remember you can't see them, so you need to listen for clues as to how they are feeling.

- On the telephone, you cannot see the other person, and they cannot see you. Always remember this, and try to sound friendly, approachable, professional and all the other things you would like them to see if they could see you. Try visualising them sat facing you, and speak as you would to their face.

- Transfer calls as little as possible—always try to deal with things if you can, because most people hate being transferred. If you have to transfer a call, tell the customer who you are putting them through to. In addition, if you can, tell the recipient of the call a little about the customer, to avoid them having to repeat themselves.

COMMUNICATING WITH PEOPLE IN WRITING

Letters have three main functions:

- to give information
- to get information
- to get something done.

They also need to create in the mind of the reader the impression that the writer and their organisation are efficient, helpful, professional and polite. Always ensure your letters are not only accurate but also written with the right tone.

Who are you writing to?

You don't always know who you are writing to. That is, you don't always know their age, language or intelligence. They may know about your organisation, or they may not. You need to take this into account, and write clearly and simply, without using technical terms, jargon or abbreviations.

When to write
- Always write promptly.
- Write when it is more appropriate than telephoning or seeing the person.
- Write when you have information they need.
- Write when you want to ask questions.

What do people want to know in a letter?
- Who it is from (your name, nor just your job title).
- Where it is from.
- Where to reply to.
- When to reply by.
- Who to telephone in case of query.

Signs of a good letter
- A heading saying what the letter is about.
- An introduction.
- Broken into short paragraphs.
- Clear, simple writing.
- Concluded with a summary of what the recipient needs to do.
- Gives the impression the writer knows what they are talking about.
- Gives a good image of the organisation.
- Short and to the point—not padded out with irrelevant information.
- Smart—no mistakes or corrections.
- Polite.
- Truthful.
- Written in a logical order.

QUESTIONS AND ANSWERS

My work only ever deals with internal customers. Is customer care really that important for me?
Yes. Every manager has customers, whether internal or external. For some departments, such as sales or marketing, dealing with external customers is a major part of their job. Other managers, in what we call **service departments** (such as personnel, finance and computing) only deal with internal customers. But service departments are there to service the other departments. And without that service, sales and marketing, and other departments that regularly deal with

external customers, cannot do their job. They can't provide good service to *their* customers.

So how can I improve customer care?
By setting a good example, and setting high standards for your staff. Be **proactive**. This means taking the initiative, and not waiting to be asked to do things. You could set standards for responses. Ideas for this would be:

- answering telephones within four rings
- answering all letters or memos within five days
- answering telephone messages within two days etc.

HANDLING COMPLAINTS

Complaints worry most people. However, they give us feedback from customers, so we can make improvements. Thus, we can use them to improve our customer care.

Two things are needed for handling complaints:

- a good attitude
- good procedures.

Developing a good attitude

- Be responsible.

- Do not respond aggressively.

- Don't be defensive.

- Establish the facts, by asking questions where necessary.

- Give the complainant time to express how they feel.

- If necessary, help them express themselves.

- Keep any promises you make, and don't make any you can't keep.

- Listen actively.

- Never assign blame—people don't want to know whose fault it is, they just want to know what you are going to do about it.

- Never just say 'no'—always explain.

- Respond as soon as possible.

- Show interest.

- Stay calm.

- Stay objective.

- Tell the customer what you are going to do about the complaint.

Developing good procedures
- Even if the customer is right, don't undermine your staff.

- If you have to overrule a member of staff, explain why, so they don't feel undermined.

- Give people authority to handle complaints where they need it.

- Have clear procedures.

- Make sure the procedures are known by all staff.

- Record all complaints so you can see any patterns.

APPRECIATING CONSUMER LEGISLATION

If you sell or receive goods on behalf of your organisation, you need to know what your legal rights and obligations are.

Understanding contracts
When someone buys something from someone else, they are entering into a **contract**. This contract has two parts. The first part is the customer's offer to buy at a certain price. The second part is the supplier's acceptance of the order and/or agreement to sell.

When both parts are completed, we say there is a **binding contract**. This simply means that neither party can change their minds or alter the contract terms.

Knowing about the legislation
Three Acts form the relevant legislation in England and Wales (the legislation in Scotland and Northern Ireland is slightly different).

These Acts are:

- Sale of Goods Act 1979
- Trade Descriptions Act 1968
- Consumer Protection Act 1987.

The Sale of Goods Act 1979
Goods must be:

- as described
- of merchantable quality
- fit for the purpose for which they are intended.

If goods fail to comply
If goods do not comply with all the three criteria, the purchaser is entitled to a refund.

- The seller does not have to offer anything but a cash refund, but the buyer can accept a replacement or repair if offered.

- The buyer does not have to accept a credit note.

- 'No refund' notices are illegal.

- Second-hand goods are covered by the Act, but refunds depend on a number of things like age of item, price paid etc.

- Sale items are included, but if the price was reduced because of damage, the buyer cannot later complain about that damage.

- The buyer does not legally have to produce a receipt, but the buyer can be asked for proof of purchase, e.g. cheque stub, credit card slip etc.

- The buyer is not entitled to a refund if they change their mind, decide that something does not fit, or damage the item themselves.

- The buyer is not entitled to a refund if they were aware of the fault or should have seen it, or if they did not purchase the item themselves.

The Trade Descriptions Act 1968
This relates to false descriptions of goods. A seller who gives a false description of goods is breaking the law.

The Consumer Protection Act 1987
This Act covers two offences. Firstly, sellers cannot give misleading information about prices. Secondly, goods cannot be supplied which are not reasonably safe.

CHECKLIST

- Be attentive to people:
  —listen
  —ask questions
  —take notes
  —concentrate
  —don't interrupt.

- Be proactive:
  —volunteer information
  —offer a choice wherever possible
  —point out things people may not have noticed.

- Be accurate:
  —never guess
  —find out information you don't know
  —use people's names wherever possible
  —know the law—and keep within it.

CASE STUDIES

Bev deals with an angry relative
Sheila, one of Bev's care assistants, answers the phone one morning. It is a resident's sister, asking for some information about her brother. Sheila puts her on hold, while she goes and finds Bev. By the time Bev has got back to answer the phone, the caller is very angry. 'I'm calling from a phone box!' she says, irritably. 'I never even had a chance to say what it was I wanted before she put me on hold. I could have called back if I'd known it would take so long for someone to come back to me! As it was, I kept putting more money in, expecting someone to speak to me at any minute!'
  Bev apologises for taking so long. Sheila should have asked whether

the caller was happy to hold or not. If not, she could either have taken the caller's number and got Bev to return her call, or she could have suggested the caller phone back in a few minutes. Bev should have trained her staff in telephone procedures.

Nikki neglects her internal customers

Nikki receives a memo from marketing. At the same time, she receives a request for some financial information from a credit company, and two customer complaints. She deals with the credit company first, as they are acting on behalf of many customers. Then she processes the information for the complaints. Last, she turns to the memo and the information it requested. By the time she has produced it, she has already had several phone calls, asking where the information is. Eventually, the information leaves Nikki's office two days after she received the request. Unfortunately, it is too late, and the company who have been dealing with marketing decide to give their business to somebody else.

If only Nikki had remembered that internal customers are as important as external ones—sometimes more, because they may need something from you to service customers of their own, which takes longer without you keeping them waiting.

Mike undermines his staff

Sam has a complaint about some information she has supplied to a manager in another department. She is unable to resolve it on the telephone, and the manager says he will take it up with Mike, her boss. She tells Mike what has happened, and he promises to deal with it. When the manager arrives later that day, Sam again tries to resolve the situation, but he wants to speak to Mike. Mike comes and speaks to him, and agrees that it will be put right. He also apologises for the 'mistake'.

When the other manager has gone, he says 'Sorry, Sam. I know you were in the right, but I needed to smooth things over, all right?' 'No it isn't!' Sam snaps. 'You made me look small and stupid! What's the point in me dealing with things if you just come and back down and give in to whatever other people want, as if I was in the wrong in the first place?'

If only Mike had remembered not to undermine his staff when dealing with complaints. He should have explained that Sam was in the right, but that he would put things right, to please the other manager, without undermining Sam and making it difficult for her to be seen as professional by the other manager again.

DISCUSSION POINTS

1. Think of a time when you have had poor delivery of goods or services as an internal customer from people within your organisation. What went wrong and why? Do you cause similar problems to your internal customers? What can you do about it?

2. Think of a time when you have complained. How well was your complaint handled? Are you satisfied with the way the complaint was handled? What can you learn from this about how your organisation handles complaints?

11
Managing Change

UNDERSTANDING CHANGE

Most of us live in a world of constant change. Changes in technology, employment, finance, legislation and many other things have altered the world we live and work in. Any organisation is changing all the time—the structures, systems, procedures, lines of authority and people working there are all changing.

Appreciating different types of change

Change occurs on many different scales, from small everyday changes to major changes in your organisation and how it works.

Everyday (routine) changes
These are the sort of changes that managers face every day. They are routine problem-solving exercises. This doesn't mean they don't require big decisions, or cost a lot of money, but it does mean that they are not going to change the organisation radically. Examples would be a person resigning, a machine breaking down, or a customer complaint resulting in new procedures to prevent it happening again.

Emergency changes (crises)
These are sudden crises that occur without warning and require a change to cope with them. A good example would be a strike or industrial dispute, a corporate take-over, or a supplier going out of business.

Improvement changes (innovation)
These occur all the time in good organisations, as managers see better, easier ways to do things. Examples would be new product development, introduction of computerised systems, or introduction of new procedures.

Radical changes (transformations)
This is where organisations change their entire way of doing things. This may be deliberate, or a forced response to a huge crisis. Examples would be privatisation of a public utility, a merger with another company, or closure of a large part of an organisation.

Sequence of change
Fig. 16 shows the sequence of change.

HANDLING CHANGE

When a change occurs, or you have decided a change may be necessary, and you are going to handle things yourself, a good sequence for handling change is the sequence we used for decision-making:

1. Define the problem or issue that may indicate the need for change.
2. Gather information.
3. Create options.
4. Evaluate options.
5. Decide on the best course of action: what change to make and how.
6. Implement your decision—implement the change(s).
7. Follow up and evaluate.

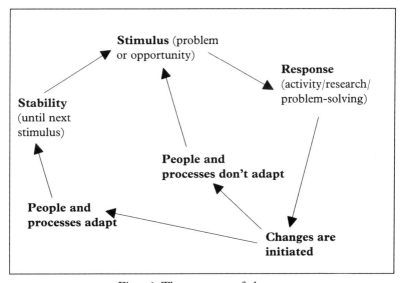

Fig. 16. The sequence of change.

QUESTIONS AND ANSWERS

So is change a good thing?
Sometimes, sometimes not. The old saying 'if it ain't broke, don't fix it' is a good one. On the other hand, just because it isn't broken, doesn't mean that things wouldn't work better after a few changes. If a change is imposed on you and it is for the worse, try to accept it—little is gained by fighting it, and your staff will probably follow your lead.

Surely people can see good change will benefit them, so there won't be any problems?
Not necessarily. Even when a change is to someone's advantage, they rarely accept it without comment. Sometimes people oppose something 'out of principle'.

Is managing change always the manager's job then?
Yes—managing is a manager's job. However, to manage change, you need to involve people and communicate, so it isn't necessary that you cope alone. Talk to people—let them know what is going on, and don't be afraid to ask for help and/or suggestions.

RESISTING CHANGE

People often resist change. How hard they resist it can be plotted on a scale, as shown in Fig. 17.

MANAGING RESISTANCE TO CHANGE

Reasons for resisting change
There are many reasons why people may resist change. If you are faced with resistance, try to discover which of them apply:

- Fear
    —of experimenting
    —of failure
    —of looking stupid
    —of loss of power
    —of loss of skills and/or expertise
    —of problems
    —of redundancy
    —of the unknown.

Fig. 17. Scale of resistance to change.

- Lack
  —of good working relationships
  —of information
  —of involvement
  —of security
  —of trust
  —of understanding of the need for change.

- Information issues
  —erroneous information
  —ignorance
  —rumours.

- Reasoning
  —clinging to the status quo—inflexibility
  —erroneous thinking
  —habit
  —historical experience
  —inability to see the benefits
  —love of conformity.

Overcoming resistance to change

You can overcome resistance to change only with effort. You need to make time for people, to try to ensure they see the change(s) in the right way.

Preparation
- Be positive.
- Check for training needs—will people need training?
- Ensure adequate resources are available to make the change go smoothly.
- Get the timing right wherever possible.
- Set clear objectives.

Information
- Be sure of your facts.
- Check things out—'look before you leap'.
- Check what things don't need to change, and make sure they aren't being affected.
- Look at things from all angles.

Involvement
- Ask for views and feedback.
- Delegate where possible—it involves people.
- Get those affected to participate in making decisions if possible.
- Get to know people.
- Involve experts. This does not have to be consultants—some of your own staff may have specialist or in-depth knowledge.

Communication
- Be honest.
- Don't withhold information—tell people as much as you can.
- Encourage two-way communication.
- Explain the circumstances that create the need for change.
- Make the change sound achievable and sensible.
- Sell people the change—don't force it on them.

Awareness

- Encourage people.
- Keep aware of the changes and how they are going.
- Recognise effort and contribution.
- Recognise that resistance is healthy and natural, and work to overcome it.
- Review and check the change works.
- Squash rumours wherever possible.

CHECKLIST

- Take time to do things properly—change takes time, and so does managing it.

- Use your strengths—use the best people where they will be best able to help you.

- Allocate enough resources—don't underestimate how long a change will take.

- Communicate.

- Involve people as early on and as extensively as possible.

CASE STUDIES

Bev's staff are unhappy about change

Bev is called in to see Matron. 'I want you to speak to your shift,' she says, 'and the other shift managers will do the same. From now on, I want the staff to work in pairs, rather than working where and when needed. This will mean that a lot of tasks will be done quicker, and quite a lot of tasks will be easier.' Bev speaks to her staff, and they don't like it. 'Don't they trust us?' says one staff member. 'I don't know,' says Bev, 'but we haven't any choice, so best to get on with it.' After a few days, Matron is displeased. The staff have been slow and everything is taking longer. If only Bev had tried to sell the change to them, so they could see why it was happening, perhaps they would have supported it more. After all, it would have made their work easier at times.

Nikki introduces a new way of handling accounts

Nikki and her team are told that the company has taken over a smaller company, and soon their accounts will be coming through Nikki's office in addition to their usual accounts. Nikki and her team can see it will be very difficult to cope with the extra figures and paperwork. Nikki sits down and tries to work out how the new workload can be managed. She decides to make each team member responsible for a stage in the processing of the new accounts. They will become practised in dealing with this stage, and will therefore become quicker.

Excitedly, she realises that all their accounts can be handled in this way, and so she explains the new system to her team. She is surprised when they all respond differently. Bill is enthusiastic, and sees the opportunity to specialise. Peter doesn't really care—he just gets on with what he's told. Jacquie isn't happy, and neither is Lyn or David. Jacquie makes a fuss, but eventually just gets on with it. Lyn and David, however, seem to be being deliberately awkward.

If only Nikki had remembered that people react differently to change, and this must be allowed for. She might also have had more success if she had consulted people and communicated with them at an earlier stage.

Mike's team suggests unnecessary changes

Mike is asked to make some changes to his accounting procedures, to fit in with the new computer system. He calls in his team and talks to them about it. They have a range of ideas, and they all discuss these. People get very enthusiastic, and the team come up with a whole package of changes, and Mike takes them to his manager. Mike's manager is less enthusiastic. 'Most of these will take time, effort and not a little money to implement, Mike,' he says, doubtfully. 'I think you'd better go back and just take care of this one—it solves the problem I originally asked you to look at.' Mike goes back to his team feeling deflated and gloomy. His team feel the same.

If things don't need to change, don't get wrapped up in enthusiasm for change, and make a lot of unnecessary changes. If changes aren't for the better, don't make them.

DISCUSSION POINTS

1. Think of the worst change you could be asked to make at work. Why does it worry you so much? What could your manager do to relieve your anxiety?

2. Identify a major change that has happened at work. How was it handled? How could it have been handled better?

12
Managing Your Career

UNDERSTANDING MANAGEMENT QUALIFICATIONS

There are many academic management qualifications which can be gained at colleges, polytechnics and universities. The most common are:

- Certificate in Management (CIM or CM)
- Certificate in Management Studies (CMS)
- Diploma in Management Studies (DMS)
- Master in Business Administration (MBA)

The entry requirements usually depend on a mixture of qualifications, management position and experience. Most of these qualifications are assessed by a mixture of coursework and examinations, to test your skills and knowledge.

NATIONAL VOCATIONAL QUALIFICATIONS

National Vocational Qualifications (NVQs) are available in many subjects, and there are NVQs in Management at Levels Three, Four and Five. The main difference between NVQs and conventional academic qualifications is that whereas academic qualifications demonstrate your skills and knowledge, NVQs show you can put this to good use in a workplace environment. They are **practical** qualifications.

NVQs are made up of different **units**. Certificates can be awarded for just one or more units, if you do not wish to take a whole NVQ.

Listed below are the NVQ units for Levels Three, Four and Five.

Management Level Three

Unit one—Maintain services and operations to meet quality standards
1.1 Maintain services and operations
1.2 Maintain the necessary conditions for an effective and safe work environment

Unit two—Contribute to the planning, monitoring and control of resources
2.1 Plan for the use of resources
2.2 Monitor and control the use of resources

Unit three—Contribute to the level of personnel
3.1 Contribute to the identification of personnel requirements
3.2 Contribute to the selection of personnel

Unit four—Contribute to the training and development of teams, individuals and self to enhance performance
4.1 Contribute to planning the training and development of teams and individuals
4.2 Contribute to training and development activities for teams and individuals
4.3 Contribute to the assessment of teams and individuals against training and development objectives
4.4 Develop oneself within the job

Unit five—Contribute to the planning, organisation and evaluation of work
5.1 Contribute to planning work activities and evaluation of work
5.2 Organise work and assist in the evaluation of work
5.3 Provide feedback on work performance to teams and individuals

Unit six—Create, maintain and enhance working relationships
6.1 Create and enhance productive working relationships with colleagues and those for whom one has supervisory responsibility
6.2 Enhance productive working relationships with one's immediate manager
6.3 Identify and minimise interpersonal conflict
6.4 Contribute to the implementation of disciplinary and grievance procedures

Unit seven—Provide information and advice for action towards meeting organisational objectives
7.1 Obtain, evaluate, record and store information
7.2 Provide information and advice

Management Level Four

Unit one—Maintain and improve service and product operations
1.1 Maintain operations to meet quality standards
1.2 Create and maintain the necessary conditions for productive work

Unit two—Contribute to the implementation of change in services, products and systems
2.1 Contribute to the evaluation of proposed changes to services, products and systems
2.2 Implement and evaluate changes to services, products and systems

Unit three—Recommend, monitor and control the use of resources
3.1 Make recommendations for expenditure
3.2 Monitor and control the use of resources

Unit four—Contribute to the recruitment and selection of personnel
4.1 Define future personnel requirements
4.2 Contribute to the assessment and selection of candidates against team and organisational requirements

Unit five—Develop teams, individuals and self to enhance performance
5.1 Develop and improve teams through planning and activities
5.2 Identify, review and improve development activities for individuals
5.3 Develop oneself within the job role

Unit six—Plan, allocate and evaluate work carried out by teams, individuals and self
6.1 Set and update work objectives for teams and individuals
6.2 Plan activities and determine work methods to achieve objectives
6.3 Allocate work and evaluate teams, individuals and self against objectives
6.4 Provide feedback to teams and individuals on their performance

Unit seven—Create, maintain and enhance effective working relationships
7.1 Establish and maintain the trust and support of one's subordinates
7.2 Establish and maintain the trust and support of one's immediate manager
7.3 Establish and maintain relationships with colleagues
7.4 Identify and minimise interpersonal conflict
7.5 Implement disciplinary and grievance procedures
7.6 Counsel staff

Unit eight—Seek, evaluate and organise information for action
8.1 Obtain and evaluate information to aid decision-making
8.2 Record and store information

Unit nine—Exchange information to solve problems and make decisions
9.1 Lead meetings and group discussions to solve problems and make decisions
9.2 Contribute to discussions to solve problems and make decisions
9.3 Advise and inform others

Management Level Five

Unit one—Initiate and implement changes and improvements in services, products and systems
1.1 Identify opportunities for improvements in services, products and systems
1.2 Evaluate proposed changes for benefits and disadvantages
1.3 Negotiate and agree the introduction of change
1.4 Implement and evaluate changes to services, products and systems
1.5 Introduce, develop and evaluate quality assurance systems

Unit two—Monitor, maintain and improve service and product delivery
2.1 Establish and maintain the supply of resources into the organisation/department
2.2 Establish and agree customer requirements
2.3 Maintain and improve operations against quality and functional specifications
2.4 Create and maintain the necessary conditions for productive work

Unit three—Monitor and control the use of resources
3.1 Control costs and enhance value
3.2 Monitor and control activities against budgets

Unit four—Secure effective resource allocation for activities and projects
4.1 Justify proposals for expenditure on projects
4.2 Negotiate and agree budgets

Unit five—Recruit and select personnel
5.1 Define future personnel requirements
5.2 Determine specifications to secure quality people
5.3 Assess and select candidates against team and organisational requirements

Unit six—Develop teams, individuals and self to enhance performance
6.1 Develop and improve teams through planning and activities
6.2 Identify, review and improve development activities for individuals
6.3 Develop oneself within the job role
6.4 Evaluate and improve the development processes used

Unit seven—Plan, allocate and evaluate work carried out by teams, individuals and self
7.1 Set and update work objectives for teams and individuals
7.2 Plan activities and determine work methods to achieve objectives
7.3 Allocate work and evaluate teams, individuals and self against objectives
7.4 Provide feedback to teams and individuals on their performance

Unit eight—Create, maintain and enhance working relationships
8.1 Establish and maintain the trust and support of one's subordinates
8.2 Establish and maintain the trust and support of one's immediate manager
8.3 Establish and maintain relationships with colleagues
8.4 Identify and minimise interpersonal conflict
8.5 Implement disciplinary and grievance procedures
8.6 Counsel staff

Unit nine—Seek, evaluate and organise information for action
9.1 Obtain and evaluate information to aid decision-making
9.2 Forecast trends and developments which affect objectives

9.3 Record and store information

Unit ten—Exchange information to solve problems and make decisions
10.1 Lead meetings and group discussions to solve problems and make decisions
10.2 Contribute to discussions to solve problems and make decisions
10.3 Advise and inform others

Note:
NVQ Units are Crown Copyright. Crown copyright is reproduced with the permission of the Controller of HMSO.

OPTIONS FOR STUDY

There are three main options:

- full-time
- part-time (day release)
- distance learning (correspondence course).

Full-time study

Advantages
- The place at which you study will probably have library, computing and other facilities for you to use.
- You may benefit from a secondment or placement with an employer.
- You will benefit from regular contact with fellow students.
- You will be able to have regular contact with your teachers.
- You can devote all your time to the course.

Disadvantages
- You will have to pay study fees and will be unable to work full-time.
- Few employers will sponsor employees on long full-time courses.
- Unless you have a work placement, you have little or no opportunity to try out your academic learning in a real workplace.

Part-time study
This is similar to full-time study, but the teaching normally occurs for one day or one afternoon and evening per week.

Advantages
- There is access to facilities.
- You can continue your job and thus protect your income.
- Many employers are happy with this sort of study, often referred to as **day release**.

Disadvantages
- There is less opportunity for group work and discussions, as time is limited.
- You need to attend regularly, so your employer will need to agree to this, unless you can attend out of working hours.
- As class time is limited, you usually need to commit yourself to a great deal of self-study, which needs discipline.

Distance learning

This is commonly known as a **correspondence course**. You buy the materials needed for study as part of your course, and work to a set programme. Most such courses also provide a tutor with whom you can correspond (hence the name correspondence courses). They will mark your work, called **assignments**.

Advantages
- You are not tied to certain times of attendance.
- No time off work is required, unless there are exams or a residential part of the course.

Disadvantages
- It can be hard to motivate yourself to study on your own.
- You lack contact with other students.
- Practical subjects such as interviewing or counselling can be difficult to cover—you can get the information, but have no opportunity to practise.

DECIDING ON OPTIONS

The following questions, if you think carefully about them, should help you decide which sort of study would be best for you.

- Does the course provide any materials?

- How many books and other things will you need to buy or have access to?

- How many people will be on the course and who are they?

- How much face-to-face contact with instructors is there?

- How much study time is required, apart from class time?

- Is there any flexibility if you have to slow down your study for a time?

- Is there any support if you are struggling with part of the course?

- What level of attendance is required?

- Who are the course teachers?

CHECKLIST

- Think carefully about what is the best qualification for you.

- Think how best to study—full-time, part-time or by distance learning.

- Look carefully at places that do the sort of course you want. Choose carefully.

Glossary

Agenda. A list of items to be discussed at a meeting.

Appraisal. A review of an employee's past, present and future performance.

Authority. The delegated power to do something.

Constraints. Factors which limit a person or situation.

Delegation. Giving some work which is normally part of your job to somebody else.

Effectiveness. Doing the right things.

Efficiency. Doing things in the right way.

Grievance. A formal complaint made by an employee against an employer.

Homeworkers. People who work from home.

Imprest. Another name for petty cash.

Induction. Initial training given when starting a new job.

Job description. A detailed record of the tasks and responsibilities of a job.

Management. Having a measure of control over resources, people, equipment, money, workloads etc.

Minutes. A written record of discussions at a meeting.

Objectivity. Looking unemotionally and logically at something.

Person specification. A detailed record of what sort of person you would like to do a job, in terms of essential and desirable criteria.

Petty cash. Cash held for minor cash purchases.

Procrastination. Putting things off until another time.

Secondment. Working in another job to gain experience.

Statutory rights. Rights given by statute or law.

Subjectivity. Looking at something and allowing our emotions to affect our perception.

Further Reading

First Time Manager, Joan Iaconetti and Patrick O'Hara (Macmillan 1985).

How to Communicate at Work, Ann Dobson (How To Books 1995).

How to Conduct Staff Appraisals, Nigel Hunt (How To Books 1994).

How to Employ and Manage Staff, Wendy Wyatt (How To Books 1995).

Managing Budgets and Cash Flows, Peter Taylor (How To Books 2nd ed. 1996).

How to Manage a Sales. Team, John Humphries (How To Books 1994).

How to Manage Computers at Work, Graham Jones (How To Books 1993).

How to Manage People at Work, John Humphries (How To Books 1995).

Introduction to Management, Malcolm Peel (Pitman 1993).

Investing in People, Harley Turnbull (How To Books 1996).

Organising Effective Training, James Chalmers (How To Books 1996).

Supervisory Studies, P. W. Betts (Pitman 1993).

Taking On Staff, David Greenwood (How To Books 1996).

Winning Presentations, Ghassan Hasbani (How To Books 1996).

Index

How To Books provide practical help on a large range of topics. They are available through all good bookshops or can be ordered direct from the distributors. Just tick the titles you want and complete the form on the following page.

___ Apply to an Industrial Tribunal (£7.99)	___ Keep Business Accounts (£7.99)
___ Applying for a Job (£7.99)	___ Know Your Rights at Work (£8.99)
___ Applying for a United States Visa (£15.99)	___ Know Your Rights: Teachers (£6.99)
___ Be a Freelance Journalist (£8.99)	___ Live & Work in America (£9.99)
___ Be a Freelance Secretary (£8.99)	___ Live & Work in Australia (£12.99)
___ Be a Local Councillor (£8.99)	___ Live & Work in Germany (£9.99)
___ Be an Effective School Governor (£9.99)	___ Live & Work in Greece (£9.99)
___ Become a Freelance Sales Agent (£9.99)	___ Live & Work in Italy (£8.99)
___ Become an Au Pair (£8.99)	___ Live & Work in New Zealand (£9.99)
___ Buy & Run a Shop (£8.99)	___ Live & Work in Portugal (£9.99)
___ Buy & Run a Small Hotel (£8.99)	___ Live & Work in Spain (£7.99)
___ Cash from your Computer (£9.99)	___ Live & Work in the Gulf (£9.99)
___ Career Planning for Women (£8.99)	___ Living & Working in Britain (£8.99)
___ Choosing a Nursing Home (£8.99)	___ Living & Working in China (£9.99)
___ Claim State Benefits (£9.99)	___ Living & Working in Hong Kong (£10.99)
___ Communicate at Work (£7.99)	___ Living & Working in Israel (£10.99)
___ Conduct Staff Appraisals (£7.99)	___ Living & Working in Japan (£8.99)
___ Conducting Effective Interviews (£8.99)	___ Living & Working in Saudi Arabia (£12.99)
___ Copyright & Law for Writers (£8.99)	___ Living & Working in the Netherlands (£9.99)
___ Counsel People at Work (£7.99)	___ Lose Weight & Keep Fit (£6.99)
___ Creating a Twist in the Tale (£8.99)	___ Make a Wedding Speech (£7.99)
___ Creative Writing (£9.99)	___ Making a Complaint (£8.99)
___ Critical Thinking for Students (£8.99)	___ Manage a Sales Team (£8.99)
___ Do Voluntary Work Abroad (£8.99)	___ Manage an Office (£8.99)
___ Do Your Own Advertising (£8.99)	___ Manage Computers at Work (£8.99)
___ Do Your Own PR (£8.99)	___ Manage People at Work (£8.99)
___ Doing Business Abroad (£9.99)	___ Manage Your Career (£8.99)
___ Emigrate (£9.99)	___ Managing Budgets & Cash Flows (£9.99)
___ Employ & Manage Staff (£8.99)	___ Managing Meetings (£8.99)
___ Find Temporary Work Abroad (£8.99)	___ Managing Your Personal Finances (£8.99)
___ Finding a Job in Canada (£9.99)	___ Market Yourself (£8.99)
___ Finding a Job in Computers (£8.99)	___ Master Book-Keeping (£8.99)
___ Finding a Job in New Zealand (£9.99)	___ Mastering Business English (£8.99)
___ Finding a Job with a Future (£8.99)	___ Master GCSE Accounts (£8.99)
___ Finding Work Overseas (£9.99)	___ Master Languages (£8.99)
___ Freelance DJ-ing (£8.99)	___ Master Public Speaking (£8.99)
___ Get a Job Abroad (£10.99)	___ Obtaining Visas & Work Permits (£9.99)
___ Get a Job in America (£9.99)	___ Organising Effective Training (£9.99)
___ Get a Job in Australia (£9.99)	___ Pass Exams Without Anxiety (£7.99)
___ Get a Job in Europe (£9.99)	___ Pass That Interview (£6.99)
___ Get a Job in France (£9.99)	___ Plan a Wedding (£7.99)
___ Get a Job in Germany (£9.99)	___ Prepare a Business Plan (£8.99)
___ Get a Job in Hotels and Catering (£8.99)	___ Publish a Book (£9.99)
___ Get a Job in Travel & Tourism (£8.99)	___ Publish a Newsletter (£9.99)
___ Get into Films & TV (£8.99)	___ Raise Funds & Sponsorship (£7.99)
___ Get into Radio (£8.99)	___ Rent & Buy Property in France (£9.99)
___ Get That Job (£6.99)	___ Rent & Buy Property in Italy (£9.99)
___ Getting your First Job (£8.99)	___ Retire Abroad (£8.99)
___ Going to University (£8.99)	___ Return to Work (£7.99)
___ Helping your Child to Read (£8.99)	___ Run a Local Campaign (£6.99)
___ Investing in People (£8.99)	___ Run a Voluntary Group (£8.99)
___ Invest in Stocks & Shares (£8.99)	___ Sell Your Business (£9.99)

___ Selling into Japan (£14.99)
___ Setting up Home in Florida (£9.99)
___ Spend a Year Abroad (£8.99)
___ Start a Business from Home (£7.99)
___ Start a New Career (£6.99)
___ Starting to Manage (£8.99)
___ Starting to Write (£8.99)
___ Start Word Processing (£8.99)
___ Start Your Own Business (£8.99)
___ Study Abroad (£8.99)
___ Study & Learn (£7.99)
___ Study & Live in Britain (£7.99)
___ Studying at University (£8.99)
___ Studying for a Degree (£8.99)
___ Successful Grandparenting (£8.99)
___ Successful Mail Order Marketing (£9.99)
___ Successful Single Parenting (£8.99)
___ Survive at College (£4.99)
___ Survive Divorce (£8.99)
___ Surviving Redundancy (£8.99)
___ Take Care of Your Heart (£5.99)
___ Taking in Students (£8.99)
___ Taking on Staff (£8.99)
___ Taking Your A-Levels (£8.99)
___ Teach Abroad (£8.99)
___ Teach Adults (£8.99)
___ Teaching Someone to Drive (£8.99)
___ Travel Round the World (£8.99)
___ Use a Library (£6.99)

___ Use the Internet (£9.99)
___ Winning Consumer Competitions (£8.99)
___ Winning Presentations (£8.99)
___ Work from Home (£8.99)
___ Work in an Office (£7.99)
___ Work in Retail (£8.99)
___ Work with Dogs (£8.99)
___ Working Abroad (£14.99)
___ Working as a Holiday Rep (£9.99)
___ Working in Japan (£10.99)
___ Working in Photography (£8.99)
___ Working in the Gulf (£10.99)
___ Working on Contract Worldwide (£9.99)
___ Working on Cruise Ships (£9.99)
___ Write a CV that Works (£7.99)
___ Write a Press Release (£9.99)
___ Write a Report (£8.99)
___ Write an Assignment (£8.99)
___ Write an Essay (£7.99)
___ Write & Sell Computer Software (£9.99)
___ Write Business Letters (£8.99)
___ Write for Publication (£8.99)
___ Write for Television (£8.99)
___ Write Your Dissertation (£8.99)
___ Writing a Non Fiction Book (£8.99)
___ Writing & Selling a Novel (£8.99)
___ Writing & Selling Short Stories (£8.99)
___ Writing Reviews (£8.99)
___ Your Own Business in Europe (£12.99)

To: Plymbridge Distributors Ltd, Plymbridge House, Estover Road, Plymouth PL6 7PZ. Customer Services Tel: (01752) 202301. Fax: (01752) 202331.

Please send me copies of the titles I have indicated. Please add postage & packing (UK £1, Europe including Eire, £2, World £3 airmail).

☐ I enclose cheque/PO payable to Plymbridge Distributors Ltd for £ [   ]

☐ Please charge to my ☐ MasterCard, ☐ Visa, ☐ AMEX card.

Account No. [ ][ ][ ][ ][ ][ ][ ][ ][ ][ ][ ][ ][ ][ ][ ][ ]

Card Expiry Date [ ][ ]19 ☎ **Credit Card orders may be faxed or phoned.**

Customer Name (CAPITALS) ....

Address ....

.... Postcode...............

Telephone........................... Signature ....

Every effort will be made to despatch your copy as soon as possible but to avoid possible disappointment please allow up to 21 days for despatch time (42 days if overseas). Prices and availability are subject to change without notice. CODE BPA